ROTTWEILER INSIGHTS

ROTTWEILER INSIGHTS

TRAINING, HEALTH, CHAOS, AND LOYALTY

THE *UNFILTERED* ROTTWEILER GUIDE

ZERO
WOOFS
GIVEN
PRESS

Rottweiler Insights

Written by Zero Woofs Given Press

Part of the Zero Woofs Dog Breed Library series

For permission requests, write to the publisher at:

Rowan's Publishing, LLC
Grass Valley, California
www.zerowoofsgiven.com
contact@zerowoofsgiven.com

Second Edition: 2025

Cover and interior design by Zero Woofs Given Press
Printed in the United States of America

Disclaimer

This book is intended for informational purposes only. It is not a substitute for professional veterinary, training, or legal advice. Always consult with qualified professionals regarding the care, training, and health of your dog.

DEDICATION

For every stubborn, slobbery, headstrong Rottweiler who's ever
ignored a command, drooled on a clean shirt, or scared the
Amazon driver half to death—
and for the humans who loved them anyway.

OTHER GUIDES AVAILABLE FROM THE ZERO WOOFS GIVEN DOG BREED LIBRARY

-Woof-a-Pedia: The Brutally Honest Dog Breed Guide
-Labrador Retriever Insights
-Great Dane Insights

BOOKS COMING SOON

-French Bulldog Insights
-German Shepherd Dog Insights
-Golden Retriever Insights
-English Bulldog Insights

TABLE OF CONTENTS

CHAPTER ONE:
A BITE OF HISTORY

History isn't trivia when it comes to Rottweilers. It's not some dusty stack of fun facts you rattle off at a pub quiz. It's the damn manual no one bothers to read—the one that explains exactly why your dog is staring at the Amazon guy like he just raided your cattle in 500 A.D. If you don't understand where this breed came from, you don't understand the breed. Period. And if you don't understand the breed, you're not fit to own one. So let's set it straight and walk through a couple thousand years of grit, muscle, and the constant PR crisis that is the Rottweiler.

People love to romanticize history. They'll coo, "Rottweilers have always been noble guardians of hearth and home," like medieval families were sitting around in drafty cottages thinking, "Gee, what we really need next to the stew pot is a dog that looks like a tax collector." Absolute bollocks. These weren't family dogs. They were employees. And employees back then didn't get dental plans. Cute didn't keep you fed. Work did.

Rottweilers were built—literally engineered by centuries of necessity, shitty roads, stubborn cattle, and markets where "reliable" meant survival. Their ancestors? The ones dragged around by the Romans while they were busy steamrolling half of Europe. Those weren't mascots. They were drover dogs. Living shock absorbers with teeth. Their entire existence was about pushing livestock down roads that looked like mud wrestling pits while thousands of hooves tried to scatter in every direction.

Imagine it: armored men stomping, shields clanging, spears rattling, cows losing their minds every time thunder cracked. Soldiers had their hands full, so the dogs had to handle the herds without flinching. The ones that collapsed under pressure didn't make it. The ones that hesitated got trampled. The ones that thought biting everything was the solution got culled. The survivors? The dogs that could read pressure, shove cattle without losing their skin, and keep moving mile after mile. Those ghosts are standing behind every Rottweiler you see today.

Fast-forward a few centuries. Rome collapses like every bloated empire eventually does. But people still need meat, which means cattle still need moving. Enter Rottweil, Germany. The butchers there saw the dogs for what they were: priceless. Not pets. Not companions. Tools. Workers. Investments with teeth.

A proper Rottweiler could drive cattle to market, hold them steady while they were being sold, and then guard the butcher's money once the day was over. Yes, the stories are true. Butchers would tie their day's earnings around the dog's neck and walk home knowing that anyone dumb enough to take a swing at them was about to regret life choices in a very loud, very toothy way. That's where the name "Rottweil Butcher's Dog" came from. Doesn't sound glamorous, right? Because it wasn't. That nickname was basically a job title.

Now people love to fluff this into folklore—like every butcher in Rottweil had some cartoonish Rottie jingling with coins around its neck, just waiting to teach a thief manners. Nope. Some did. Most didn't. But the fact that it happened at all says everything. These weren't just brutes. They were calm enough to walk through chaos and controlled enough to hold back until the moment called for violence. That balance—power with restraint—was their real currency long before kennel clubs turned it into flowery nonsense about head shapes and tan markings.

And here's where I torch some myths.

Myth one: the Rottweiler was "designed" by monks or butchers with some grand master plan. Bullshit. Nobody was drawing lineage charts by candlelight. These dogs were carved by necessity. The ones that couldn't hold up? Gone. The ones that could? They bred. That's it. No purity charts. No "careful crafting." Just brutal trial and error in a world where sentimental dogs died out.

Myth two: the breed used to be some giant softie ruined by modern times. Again—bullshit. They were never gentle giants. They weren't plush toys. They were force multipliers in dirty, loud, unpredictable environments. If anything, the modern suburban Rottie is a marshmallow compared to its ancestors, because today we've padded their world with dog parks, squeaky toys, and Instagram reels. Back then? Their jobs started at sunrise and ended when the cattle were finally penned. That's the baseline.

Then industry happened. And industry always does what it does best: replace muscle and instinct with machines. Railroads and trucks started moving livestock, and suddenly the drover's road—the crucible that built the Rottweiler—shrunk to nothing. By all rights, that should have been the death of the breed.

But it wasn't.

Because the traits that kept the breed alive—strength, nerve, presence, judgment—were still useful anywhere humans needed a steady enforcer. Draft harnesses replaced cattle drives. Yard patrols replaced markets. Night watches replaced muddy roads. You put a Rottweiler in a carting harness today and it's not nostalgia—it's history written into bone and muscle. The frame tells you everything: mass built for mileage, a chest like a forge bellows, a neck that doesn't quit, and a rear end made for pushing, not prancing. None of it is cosmetic. It's a blueprint.

As policing started professionalizing in Germany, the difference between loud dogs and reliable dogs stopped being academic. Markets were one thing. Crowds, rifles, and uniforms were another. Suddenly, it wasn't enough to look scary. These dogs had to be solid. They had to have the nerve to walk into a screaming mob and not lose it. They had to handle gunfire, chaos, and confusion without unraveling. And that's when people finally started writing things down. Standards.

Not the kind you see on breeder websites drooling over eye shape and tan points. Real standards. The kind that drew a line around what the breed had already proven it could do: steadiness, judgment, courage with brakes. Because let's be real—what good is a blocky head if the brain behind it folds at the first pistol crack? The written standard kept circling back to character. Because character is what kept butchers' coin purses safe, soldiers' gear moving, and crowds under control.

Then Europe set itself on fire. Twice.

World War I, and then the encore. And any remaining romance about "working dogs" went up in smoke with it. Dogs became whatever humans needed in the moment. Ammunition mules when the carts bogged down. Message carriers when the lines went dead. Searchers dragging through battlefields where even the moon looked hostile. Rottweilers weren't the only dogs doing this, but they did it well enough to leave a mark. And by the time the world went up again in the 1940s, their reputation for steadiness under pressure was cemented.

Not glamour. Not glory. Reliability. The one thing armies never have enough of.

And when soldiers came home, so did the stories. Some brought actual dogs with them. Others just brought memories. Either way, the Rottweiler's reputation crossed oceans. By the time they hit North America in bigger numbers, they carried baggage—some of it earned, some of it not.

Reputation travels faster than pedigrees. Before the wars, you could find a few Rottweilers scattered around North America. After the wars? Way more. They came with immigrants who valued hard dogs that didn't crumble under pressure, and with soldiers who'd seen firsthand the difference between a dog that postured and a dog that delivered.

And when they landed here, the breed met two very different types of buyers. On one side, you had the serious handlers. The ones who treated the Rottie like a partner, not a trophy. They invested in socialization, trained with consistency, and understood that presence comes with responsibility. These folks knew what they had, and they worked the dog with standards.

Then there was the other camp. The assholes. The people who wanted a walking billboard for their ego. They didn't care about stability, judgment, or partnership. They wanted 100 pounds of intimidation on a leash they barely knew how to hold. And if you're wondering which camp grew faster once the Rottweiler hit a "most popular breeds" list, I'll give you one guess.

Popularity is a bill that always comes due. And the Rottweiler paid it hard. Backyard breeders started pumping out litters like party flyers. They chased big heads, flashy markings, bulk—shit that looked good in photos but didn't mean jack when it came to nerves or judgment. Puppies got raised in pens instead of the real world they'd have to live in. Training was replaced with yelling, volume standing in for timing. What came out of those kennels looked like Rottweilers but acted like question marks.

Put a dog like that in the wrong hands—which is exactly what happened—and suddenly you've got incidents. Put those incidents in front of cameras, and now you've got headlines. And headlines travel a hell of a lot faster than truth ever does. The story wasn't about poor husbandry, bad genetics, or clueless ownership. The story was always the same: snarling black-and-tan head, scary teeth, dramatic headline, cue moral panic.

And panic turns into policy. Insurance companies started blacklisting Rottweilers. Landlords added clauses. City councils debated bans. None of those documents talked about breeder incentives, owner competence, or selection pressure. They didn't name the assholes who treated serious working dogs like props. They just named the breed. And good dogs with good owners got stuck paying the invoice.

This is where people start whining, "The breed changed." Wrong. The breed didn't change. The environment changed. The incentives changed. The handling changed. A powerful dog doesn't invent problems out of thin air—it magnifies whatever's already there. Bad breeding, bad training, bad owners. Put that in a Rottie, and you're going to see the fallout tenfold.

Meanwhile, the real dogs, the ones truest to their roots, kept showing up wherever people still respected the original job description. Handle a correct Rottweiler in a crowd and you'll feel it. Noise goes up, chaos swells, and the dog gets calmer. Head comes up, scan widens, breathing stays steady. Then, the most important part: the dog looks to you for the final call. If you're in charge, the Rottweiler accepts your decision and holds the line.

That "clause" matters. The butcher's dog had autonomy because the work demanded it. But autonomy without leadership? That's freelancing. And freelancing in a guardian breed is how little problems grow teeth. The fix isn't louder commands or macho chest-puffing. The fix is boring, practiced clarity. Rules that don't move. Consistency that becomes gospel. The butcher didn't scream over cattle pens all day. He set boundaries once and enforced them forever. That's the kind of language Rottweilers understand.

And here's the thing most people get dead wrong: they call modern Rottweilers "softened." They look at some suburban dog snoozing at the park and think it's worlds away from the cart-pulling, cattle-driving beasts of history. But what's actually softened are expectations. Some bloodlines got watered down for looks. Some owners got good at mistaking passivity for stability. But a correct Rottweiler is not dull. It's deliberate.

There's a huge difference.

A correct dog can go from flat-out asleep to decisive action in the time it takes a door to open—and then drop back to neutral before you finish the sentence. That's not "chill." That's judgment. If your Rottweiler is just a lump on the floor, that's not calm. That's "off." Calm is a state that holds even under pressure, even in motion, even when shit gets loud. That's what the old jobs bred into them: a thousand decisions under fire, every single day.

Sure, the jobs changed. Your dog isn't dragging carts of meat down dirt roads anymore or guarding coin purses in a rowdy market. Today's load is smaller: a leash, a recall, a doorbell test, a stranger at the gate. But the muscle memory underneath? Same as ever. When your Rottweiler squares up, plants its feet, and gives a stranger that steady, silent look—the one that slows their stride—you're not seeing a malfunction. You're watching history flicker to life. You're watching a job description waiting for your command.

That's the honest arc: function to function, with side quests through fashion and fear-mongering. And if you want this breed, you don't just get the cute version. You take custody of that arc. Your responsibility is to meet it halfway. Give the body purpose. Teach the brain that your judgment outranks its instincts. Socialize deliberately, not lazily. And when the old genes peek through—the stance, the stillness, the weight shift that whispers, *"I've got this"—*don't freak out, and don't strut like you're invincible. Give the dog direction. That's what it's been waiting for... for about two thousand years.

And if you still think history is just trivia, you've clearly never met a Rottweiler. This breed drags its history into your living room with muddy paws and drops it right in your lap. Every single quirk—good, bad, misunderstood— that you see in a modern Rottie is a direct echo of what kept its ancestors alive.

Suspicion of strangers? People moan, "Why won't my Rottie greet guests like a Golden?" Because it wasn't bred to. For centuries, its job was to look at outsiders and say, "Prove you belong here." That doesn't evaporate just because you'd like your neighbors to be greeted with butt wiggles. If you wanted everyone-loving sunshine, you should've bought a Labrador. You didn't. You bought a Rottweiler. Own it.

Same with power. These dogs are strong enough to knock you on your ass without trying. That's not an accident of genetics—it's a leftover from muscling cattle through chaos. Pretend that body doesn't exist, and you'll find out the hard way when your dog hits the end of the leash and drags you across the yard after a squirrel.

And loyalty? Everyone gushes about how "loyal" Rottweilers are, but nobody finishes the sentence. Loyal to one person. Historically, that's what the butcher needed: a shadow. Not a social butterfly. That's why modern Rotties can be velcro dogs—clingy with their chosen human and downright dismissive of everyone else. Some owners eat that up. Others panic when the dog growls at their in-laws. But that's not a defect. That's history wagging its tail.

Then comes the big one: reputation.

For centuries, Rottweilers were invisible workhorses. Then, in the 1980s and 90s, the breed got drafted into a role it never asked for: media scapegoat. The "dangerous dog" circus rolled through, and Rottweilers got tossed in with Dobermans and Pit Bulls. Sensational headlines sold papers. "Killer Dog Mauls Child" is a lot juicier than "Idiot Owner Leaves Untrained Working Breed Alone With Kids." And so a dog that once hauled carts and protected butchers got painted as a monster.

And that image stuck. Landlords banned them. Insurance companies blacklisted them. Strangers crossed the street. None of it was about the breed standard. The dogs didn't suddenly wake up one morning more vicious. They just got handed to the wrong people—the ones who saw muscle as an ego boost instead of a responsibility. And, spoiler alert: bad humans ruin good dogs. Always have. Always will.

Here's the tricky part though. Rottweilers aren't saints. They're not misunderstood angels who've just been unfairly labeled. They're not Labradors with a PR problem. A poorly bred, poorly trained Rottie is a walking lawsuit waiting to happen. They're not forgiving dogs. Screw up their socialization, and they'll carry that suspicion forever. Slack off on training, and their size will amplify your failure until it's a headline. Their strength and confidence are why they're phenomenal in the right hands—and absolute disasters in the wrong ones. That's not slander. That's the truth carved into their bones by history: high reward, high risk.

But here's the part people miss. This breed is also one of the most versatile dogs alive. Those Roman drover instincts didn't just vanish—they evolved. They turned into police work. Into military service. Into therapy dog programs. Into search and rescue. Into competitive obedience and protection sports. Into goofy family guardians who nap with toddlers and steal couch cushions when nobody's looking. That's the magic of the Rottweiler: the same traits that make them intimidating can also make them phenomenal, if—and this is a fucking mountain-sized if— the human on the other end of the leash is up to the task.

Think about it. You've got a dog with raw muscle, suspicion, brains, and presence. That combo can be terrifying if it's in the wrong hands, but in the right hands, it's a masterpiece. That's why you'll see Rotties hauling kids in carts at breed demos, passing therapy dog exams, competing in high-level obedience, and then turning around and running a patrol shift or pulling a sled. They're not one-trick ponies. They're Swiss Army knives in dog form. But again—the knife doesn't decide how it's used. The handler does.

Modern Rottweilers are basically walking history lessons. Every time you look at one, you're staring at the blueprint of a working animal shaped by utility, not cuteness. They weren't built for Instagram. They weren't built for your HOA's idea of "a nice family dog." They were built for work. Forged in survival. Hardened by demand. That's why they are not for everyone. If you want easy, go buy a stuffed animal. If you want a Rottweiler, accept that you're inheriting every ounce of grit, suspicion, strength, and loyalty that history baked into their DNA.

And here's the blunt truth: if more people respected the history, fewer Rotties would end up dumped in rescues. Too many folks march into a breeder's yard or, worse, a backyard litter thinking they're buying a teddy bear with teeth. Then the dog grows up, shows its genetic cards, and suddenly they're shocked when the sweet fluffball doesn't love strangers, has opinions about boundaries, and weighs enough to drag them across the yard like a cheap lawn ornament. What do they do? They bail. And that's how you end up with Rottweilers in shelters labeled "aggressive" when really they're just confused, under-socialized, and owned by people who didn't have the balls to learn what they were actually getting into.

History matters. It's not trivia. It's the operating manual. It's the reason your dog doesn't welcome strangers with kisses, the reason it can flatten you by accident, the reason it sticks to one person like Velcro and couldn't care less about the rest. None of that is broken. None of that is a mistake. That's the fucking breed.

So let's be blunt. You didn't buy a Golden Retriever. You didn't buy a Labrador. You didn't buy a doodle with jazz hands. You bought a Rottweiler. Which means you bought two thousand years of survival instincts, muscle, judgment, suspicion, and loyalty sharpened into a weapon that only works properly with the right handler.

You either respect that history, or you're going to fight against it every single day. And when people fight against what a dog was bred to be, the dog always loses. That's why this chapter exists. That's why this book exists. Not to sell you a sugar-coated dream of a gentle giant. Not to hand you breeder-approved bedtime stories. But to tell you the goddamn truth about Rottweilers: what they were, what they are, and what they will always be.

If you want one, then step the fuck up. Because this breed has been waiting for your direction for two thousand years.

Chapter Two:
Understanding Your Rottweiler

There's a reason people who actually know Rottweilers smirk when they hear somebody say, "Oh, I had a German Shepherd, so I know what to expect." Wrong. Or worse, "I grew up with a Pit Bull, so a Rottie's basically the same, right?" Wrong again. Try again. You could stack ten Shepherds and ten Pits together and still not get the creature you just brought home. A Rottweiler isn't some interchangeable "tough dog" you can swap out like batteries. They're their own goddamn brand of chaos. A cocktail mixed with brute strength, clingy affection, razor-wire suspicion, and a stubborn streak that makes your average toddler look like a pushover.

Living with a Rottweiler is like hosting a revolving cast of characters in your house: bodyguard, toddler, drunk roommate, all rolled into one. And here's the kicker—sometimes all three show up in the same hour. You're sitting there drinking coffee, and suddenly you've got a watchdog glaring at the mailman, a whiny toddler climbing into your lap, and a slobbering drunk burping in your ear while snoring like a busted chainsaw. That's not three dogs. That's one Rottweiler, before lunch.

At their core, Rottweilers are contradictions on four legs. They're loyal in a way that feels almost obsessive—once they've decided you're their human, congratulations, you now own a 100-pound shadow. This shadow doesn't politely lurk in the corner either. It parks itself outside your shower. It escorts you to the bathroom. It follows you into the kitchen like you're about to perform some Michelin-star culinary masterpiece just for them. You will trip over this dog. You will beg this dog for space. You will whisper "for fuck's sake, give me five minutes" at least once a day.

But loyalty isn't the whole story. It's layered with suspicion so strong it borders on paranoia. That Velcro love comes with constant side-eye at the rest of the world. You think you're out for a coffee run. Your Rottweiler thinks you're leading a presidential convoy through enemy territory. Every passing stranger is a question mark. Every car door slamming three blocks away gets logged in their mental database. You're humming along to the radio, and your Rottie's already running threat assessments like a furry Secret Service agent.

That mix—clingy affection glued to nightclub-bouncer suspicion—is what makes this breed both brilliant and a royal pain in the ass. Nail the balance, and you've got a partner who will love you harder than you thought possible while doubling as the safest alarm system on four legs. Screw it up, and you've basically adopted a paranoid stalker who thinks your friends are home invaders and has a meltdown every time you leave the house without them. With Rottweilers, the stakes aren't low. You don't just coast along and hope for the best.

Suspicion is baked into their DNA. These dogs weren't bred to wait around for someone to say "good boy" before stepping in. They were bred to notice, to decide, to act if necessary. That's what made them such damn good drovers and guardians in the first place. But that also means when you're at the door, laughing and hugging a long-lost buddy, your Rottie isn't automatically convinced. They're silently doing math: friend or foe? Guest or intruder? Should I let this person in, or should I plant them in the drywall?

And this is not a Labrador we're talking about. They're not living by the gospel of "every stranger is a best friend waiting to happen." They don't fling themselves belly-first at whoever wanders up. A Rottweiler greets the world with a poker face and a mental checklist. Who are you? Why are you here? Do I need to do something about it? It's not "mean," it's not "antisocial"—it's just their wiring.

Now, before you start sweating bullets and wondering if you've brought home a furry paranoia machine, let's level it out. Because for all that suspicion, Rottweilers are also shockingly sensitive. Not delicate. Not fragile. Emotionally tuned in. They can read you like you're written in giant block letters. The tone of your voice, the set of your shoulders, the sigh you let out when the day's been crap—

they pick it all up. Where another dog is busy sniffing lampposts, a Rottie is scanning your emotional weather report.

And that's where the "soulmate" talk comes from. Not in some glittery Hallmark way, but in the unnerving way where your dog already knows what you're feeling before you've even sorted it out yourself. You don't have to speak. You don't even have to move. They know. Sometimes it feels like magic. Sometimes it's creepy as hell. But it's always intense.

This is also where the Velcro reputation really shows itself. Forget "majestic working dog" imagery—your Rottie thinks personal space is a myth invented by cat owners. That ninety-pound body that could plow a cart through town? It'll happily fold itself into your lap like a Chihuahua, roll belly-up, and snore so loud you'll have to crank Netflix just to hear what the hell's happening on screen.

And it doesn't stop when you stand up. You go to the kitchen? They're at your heels. You go to the bathroom? They're stationed outside like they've been assigned guard duty. Crawl into bed? Congratulations, you've just adopted a drooling space heater that thinks pressing into your spine is a birthright. These dogs want you. Not the next room. Not the yard. Not the overpriced bed you bought. You.

But here's the danger: leave them alone too long, and that Velcro devotion goes sour. It starts small. Pacing. Whining. Sighing. Then the escalation hits. Shoes shredded. Couch cushions massacred. Drywall chipped like someone took a chisel to it. A Rottweiler left too long isn't quietly gazing out the window waiting for you. They're staging their own version of Fight Club in your living room. Ignore their need for closeness, and you've got yourself a behavioral hurricane faster than you can Google "Rottweiler separation anxiety" at two in the morning.

And yet—clingy doesn't mean weak. Because right next to that desperate attachment lives a streak of stubborn independence that could drive a saint to drinking. This is not a Golden Retriever wagging and waiting for your approval. This is a dog who will look you dead in the eye, listen carefully, and then decide, "Yeah… no thanks."

Training a Rottweiler isn't training in the classic sense. It's negotiation. It's like trying to convince a three-year-old to eat broccoli when the kid has already lawyered up. They'll test you. They'll stall. They'll stare. They'll see if you actually mean what you say. And if you don't? Game over. From that point on, you're background noise and they're in charge.

This is where people get whiplash with the breed. One minute, your Rottweiler is plastered to your hip like a magnet. The next, you give a command and they stare at you like you've just suggested something beneath them. It's not random. It's not disobedience for fun. It's calculation. These dogs weren't bred to be drones; they were bred to think. And sometimes the problem they decide needs solving is you.

And here's where the public embarrassment factor comes in, because Rottweilers have a special gift for making you look like an idiot. Picture it: you're at the park, people are watching, and you tell your dog to sit. A Golden Retriever would plop its butt down so fast it might sprain something, tail wagging like it just solved world hunger. Your Rottie? They'll stand there blinking at you, maybe tilt their head, maybe look past you like something on the horizon is more interesting. And you know what's happening? Everyone's watching. Suddenly you're not the responsible adult with the badass dog—you're the clown who can't control their "danger breed."

And here's the dangerous part: if your Rottweiler figures out you don't mean what you say, that lesson sets in like wet cement. Next thing you know, you've got a 100-pound lawyer cross-examining your every command. Did you really mean sit? Or is this more of a suggestion? Because if it's a suggestion, they're happy to decline. And once you've taught them that your words are optional? Good luck taking that habit back when it actually matters.

See, Rottweilers don't grovel. They don't pant and beg for approval. They don't live to make you happy. They'll work for you—sure—but only if they've bought into the deal. If you're boring, they'll check out. If you're inconsistent, they'll outsmart you. If you let them win a little battle, they'll start strategizing how to win the war. And don't fool yourself, they're keeping score. These aren't Labradors out to win "teacher's pet." They're the sharp kid in class who already knows the material and spends the whole semester proving they're smarter than the teacher.

Which is why training a Rottweiler feels less like obedience and more like ongoing contract negotiations. Do I respect you enough to do this your way? Or am I going to solve the problem myself? Sometimes, the problem they've decided to solve is you.

And here's where new owners really stumble, because they confuse clinginess with pliability. They think, "Oh, my dog never leaves my side, they must be desperate to please me." Wrong. They're desperate to be with you, not desperate to obey you. Those are two very different things. Loyalty does not equal submission. You'll get endless love, sure. You'll get attachment so strong you can't pee in peace. But respect? Respect you have to earn, and keep earning.

Now let's pause and talk about the three classic Rottweiler owner archetypes—the ones who fail spectacularly.

First, the pushover. Sweet, loving, maybe even well-intentioned. They give commands like they're asking a question. "Sit? Stay? Maybe? Please?" The Rottweiler hears this and translates it into "Do whatever the hell you want." Within months, this household has been annexed. The dog is running things, the furniture is destroyed, and the pushover is crying on Facebook asking why their "sweet puppy" turned into a monster.

Second, the chaos human. This is the person who can't get their own life together but thought bringing home a Rottweiler was a good idea. Newsflash: your dog is a mirror. If you're anxious, inconsistent, or a hot mess, your Rottweiler is going to be a hot mess squared. You think you're teaching them? Wrong again. They're reading you, and if you're all over the place, they'll reflect it back bigger and louder. These are the folks who wind up with a neurotic, destructive dog because they couldn't manage themselves first.

And finally, the wannabe alpha. This guy watched a few bad TV shows, read some outdated pack-leader garbage, and thinks he's going to dominate his Rottweiler into submission. Newsflash number two: Rottweilers aren't impressed by cosplay. They'll tolerate you stomping around like you're king of the wolves for about five minutes, and then they'll look at you like you're a joke. You don't scare them. You don't impress them. You just look ridiculous. And in the meantime, you've probably damaged their trust. Congrats, you're not a leader—you're just an ass.

Now let's swing back to the flip side of their personality—the emotional intelligence. Because this is the part that catches even seasoned dog people off guard. A Rottweiler doesn't just stick to you physically; they tune into you emotionally like they've hacked your nervous system. You raise your voice at your kid? Your Rottie slinks off like you just scolded them. You cry at the kitchen table? They'll press that giant head into your chest like they can soak up your sadness. Try to fake being "fine" when you're not? Forget it. You can fool your boss, your therapist, and half your friends, but you cannot lie to a Rottweiler.

Sounds magical, right? Like living with a four-legged soulmate? Sure. But it's also a trap. Because that emotional radar doesn't turn off. When you're anxious, they're anxious. When you're pissed, they're tense. When you're inconsistent, they're confused. They don't just follow your mood—they magnify it. Which means if you're a mess, your Rottweiler is going to be a bigger mess. And that's where things go sideways.

Here's the part no sugarcoated breed guide wants to admit: a Rottweiler that senses weakness in their human doesn't go soft. They step up. They get pushy. They get reactive. Sometimes they even get aggressive, because in their mind, somebody has to take control, and if it's not you, it sure as hell is going to be them. It's not because they're "bad dogs." It's because they're wired to fill the leadership vacuum. You're not steering the ship? Fine. They'll grab the wheel. Straight into the rocks.

And this is what I mean when I say they expose every crack in you. Your patience. Your consistency. Your emotional state. You can bluff your way through life in a lot of areas, but not with this breed. They'll force you to face your own bullshit whether you like it or not. Sometimes they'll make you better. Sometimes they'll just make you miserable. Often both.

Which circles back to one of the most dangerous myths about Rottweilers: that they're basically the same as German Shepherds or Pit Bulls. No. Absolutely not. That thinking is how people wind up on the evening news. Each of those breeds is its own loaded weapon, with its own quirks and wiring. Treating them like interchangeable "guard dogs" is like mixing up a scalpel, a chainsaw, and a grenade. Technically all tools, sure. But you'd better know the difference before you pick one up.

German Shepherds? Soldiers. Brilliant, driven, eager for orders. Always asking "What's next, boss?" But also neurotic as hell if you don't handle them right. Their energy is a live wire, sparking all over the place.

Pit Bulls? They're clowns with muscles. People-obsessed to the point of absurdity. Loyal, goofy, stubborn, tenacious. But suspicious of strangers? Not usually. A Pit Bull will welcome your shady neighbor's sketchy friend into your house with a tail wag and a grin.

Now the Rottweiler. They're methodical. Calculating. They don't waste energy. They sit back, size things up, and then make one decisive move when it counts. A Shepherd barks at everything. A Pit Bull wags at everything. A Rottie sits in silence until the line is crossed—and then unleashes hell. That's not a minor difference. That's the difference between a warning shot and a sledgehammer.

And if you can't see why that matters, you're not ready for one.

Now, let's ground this whole paradox in something you'll absolutely live through: the Velcro Dog phase. And by "phase," I mean lifestyle, because some Rotties never grow out of it.

Here's the short version: your bathroom is no longer private. You try to shut the door, and they're on the other side sighing like you've betrayed them. Your hallway? A tripping hazard, because your 100-pound shadow is always glued to your heels. Leave the house without them? You'll get the Abandonment Opera—moaning, howling, full Broadway performance—as if you've just vanished into witness protection. Bedtime? Forget personal space. They'll press themselves against you so hard you'll be sweating and claustrophobic before midnight. Work from home? They'll sit through every Zoom call, sighing like you're boring the hell out of them, but refusing to leave the room.

And if you botch crate training? You'll discover exactly how much noise, force, and creativity a Rottweiler can put into a prison break. Chewing, digging, howling—it's like watching Shawshank Redemption on four legs.

Some people laugh this off as "cute quirks." And sure, it's hilarious at first. But here's the warning: if you don't channel that attachment, you're creating a clingy, anxious wreck who can't function without you. Translation: destroyed furniture, drywall carnage, angry neighbors, and a dog who screams bloody murder every time you buy groceries.

And that's just inside the house. Out in the real world, the contradictions hit even harder. Picture the UPS driver. To you, he's a friendly guy dropping off your Amazon splurge. To your Rottweiler, he's a suspicious figure approaching the territory with a giant box. Now multiply that instinct by about ten if the driver dares to walk up when you're not home. Rottweilers don't bark for fun; when they do, it's usually because they've already made up their mind.

Or let's talk about family gatherings. Everyone's laughing, music's playing, the wine is flowing—and your dog is in the corner, poker-faced, scanning Uncle Steve like he's a potential intruder. Doesn't matter if you've known Steve for thirty years. Your Rottie doesn't care about family trees; they care about body language. And if Uncle Steve stumbles over drunk and gives you an over-enthusiastic hug? Well, congratulations, now you're explaining to your relatives why the "sweet family dog" just stepped between you like a bouncer at closing time.

Dog parks? Oh, buckle up. This is where the stubborn independence and suspicion combo can blow up in your face. A Shepherd will herd, a Pit Bull will play rough, but a Rottweiler will size up every dog in the park before deciding how to react. Some will ignore the chaos. Others will decide they've been promoted to "sheriff" and start breaking up scuffles—sometimes with more force than you wanted. And if you're not in control? You're the headline in tomorrow's neighborhood Facebook group.

Now, does this mean living with a Rottweiler is nothing but drama? No. What it means is that you can't coast. You can't half-ass it. These dogs are either your greatest ally or your biggest liability, depending entirely on how consistent you are.

Here's the brutal truth most people don't want to hear: understanding a Rottweiler isn't about memorizing some tidy bullet list of "breed traits." It's about living with contradictions every damn day. They're clingy but stubborn. Loyal but suspicious. Affectionate but controlling. Smart but selective. And if that sounds exhausting, it's because sometimes it is.

But—here's the payoff. If you earn it, if you prove yourself, if you hold your ground without being an ass, a Rottweiler will give you a kind of devotion no other breed can match. Not pet devotion. Not "family dog" devotion. I'm talking about ride-or-die, in-the-trenches, "bury me next to my human" devotion. The kind of loyalty that makes you feel like you've got a partner in life, not just a pet.

It's not glamorous. It's not easy. It's not even fun all the time. But for the rare human who can shoulder the clinginess, the stubborn streak, and the emotional mirror they shove in your face, the reward is worth every headache.

Because a Rottweiler isn't just a dog. They're your shadow. Your bodyguard. Your therapist. Your occasional source of public humiliation. And yes, sometimes your biggest pain in the ass.

So if what you really want is a Golden Retriever in a black-and-tan suit, walk away now. You'll hate every second. But if you want the raw, unfiltered truth of dog ownership in one slobber-slinging, muscle-packed, chaos-fueled package? Then buckle the hell up. Because life with a Rottweiler? That's as real as it gets.

CHAPTER THREE:

THE ROLE OF GENETICS IN BEHAVIOR AND HEALTH

If you think your Rottweiler's quirks, temper tantrums, or genius-level manipulation are entirely because of how you raise them—newsflash: you're only holding half the damn deck. The other half was already stacked before you ever picked your puppy out of the litter. That's genetics. Training, environment, and daily structure matter like hell, but your Rottie's DNA is the foundation. And if the foundation is cracked, you're not building a mansion—you're slapping wallpaper over rot.

People love the phrase "nature versus nurture." It's catchy. Sounds like a debate. But it's not a versus. It's a tag-team. Genes load the gun. Environment pulls the trigger. You can raise your Rottweiler in a loving home, buy the fancy food, hire the trainer, and give them organic kale cookies—but if the pup comes from garbage bloodlines, you're fighting uphill every single day. And uphill against a dog bred like a tank? That's a losing game.

Here's where it gets real: temperament is heritable. That loyalty, suspicion, stamina, even the stubborn streak that makes you want to pour whiskey in your morning coffee— it's all wired in. You're not just buying a puppy; you're buying a family tree. That sharp-eyed, quick-to-bark pup? Chances are dad was a neighborhood alarm system. The one who plants her ass and stares you down in a battle of wills? Her mom probably still runs her household like a mafia boss.

And unlike other breeds, where "bad genetics" might give you nothing worse than a scatterbrained retriever or a lazy hound, bad genetics in a Rottweiler are a whole different beast. Faulty wiring in a Rottie doesn't mean "oops, he chases squirrels." It means unpredictable nerves, unstable aggression, or worse: a lack of inhibition. Combine 120 pounds of muscle with zero brakes, and congratulations— you're not holding a leash, you're holding liability.

The good side? When genetics *do* line up right, it's magic. That's when you get the unicorn: the calm, confident dog who doesn't blink at fireworks, but who will plant himself between you and a stranger without hesitation. The athlete who can hike for hours, then crash on the couch without destroying it. The steady, intuitive protector who reads you like a diary but doesn't make every goddamn shadow into a conspiracy. That's the payoff of sound breeding—it sets the baseline that nurture can polish.

But let's clear something up: genetics are tendencies, not destiny. A naturally protective dog raised with boundaries and exposure? That's your dream guardian. The same dog raised in chaos and ignorance? That's your nightmare lawsuit. You don't get to rewrite DNA—but you do get to steer it. Think of genetics as a river. You can't change where it starts, but you can influence where it flows.

Still, pretending nurture alone can fix bad breeding is the biggest lie in the dog world. If a breeder pairs two unstable, reactive dogs with hips held together by duct tape and sells the litter to unsuspecting buyers, no amount of puppy classes or positive affirmations will turn that pup into Lassie. What you'll get is heartbreak, stress, and possibly danger. You'll be the one crying on the kitchen floor Googling "Rottweiler aggression at 9 months" while your dog chews through the drywall.

And here's the gut punch: unstable temperament doesn't "grow out" of a dog. Nervy puppies become nervy adults. Fearful moms make fearful litters. Aggressive dads pass on more than just their scowl. Socialization helps, structure helps, training helps—but only if the genetic wiring is stable enough to support it. Otherwise, you're just trying to duct tape over a cracked foundation.

If temperament is one loaded weapon in your Rottweiler's DNA, health is the other. And spoiler alert—the safety's off. This isn't just about minor inconveniences. With a breed this physically powerful, bad genetics don't mean "a limp here or there." They mean pain, heartbreak, and lives cut short. They mean the difference between ten solid years with your best friend or saying goodbye while they're still in their prime.

Let's start with the classic: hip and elbow dysplasia. You've probably seen the words stamped on breeder websites—"OFA Certified," "PennHIP tested." That's not marketing fluff. That's survival. Dysplasia happens when the joints don't form correctly, and the result is arthritis, chronic pain, and lameness. And here's the kicker: it's heritable. If both parents have weak hips, Junior isn't winning the lottery—he's inheriting the family curse.

A Rottweiler with bad hips is more than a sad sight—it's a tragedy. This is a breed designed to pull carts, drive cattle, and stand their ground. When their skeleton betrays them, you don't just lose a dog—you lose the essence of the breed. And don't let breeders blow smoke up your ass with "it skips generations." No, it doesn't. The only way dysplasia gets reduced is when breeders aggressively screen, ruthlessly cut unfit dogs out of programs, and stop pretending that "two cute dogs" equals a breeding plan.

Now, let's move north—to the heart. Rottweilers are heartbreakers in the most literal sense. Sub-aortic stenosis (SAS) is a narrowing of the aorta that forces the heart to work overtime. The results? Fainting spells, murmurs, or the worst of all—sudden death. Yeah, sudden. As in: you think your dog's healthy, you're on a walk, and they collapse before you can even react. This isn't rare. It's genetic. And unless breeders are doing echocardiograms and screening their stock, you're back at Russian roulette, only now the gun's pointed at your best friend's chest.

The cruelest part about SAS? Sometimes you don't know until it's too late. No warning, no buildup. One day you've got a thriving young dog, the next you're standing in the ER while a vet shakes their head. That's the reality of ignoring heart testing. If your breeder can't even spell "echocardiogram," run.

And then there's the monster lurking in the shadows: cancer. Specifically, osteosarcoma—bone cancer. Rottweilers top the charts for it. Aggressive. Relentless. One limp can spiral into a diagnosis that ends with amputation, chemo, and a countdown you didn't sign up for. This isn't scare-tactic crap—it's statistics. And unlike hips or hearts, there's no scan that magically clears the line. What responsible breeders *can* do is track family histories, avoid doubling up on lines heavy with cancer, and make informed choices. What backyard breeders do? Shrug and say, "All dogs get sick."

And don't get me started on longevity. A well-bred Rottweiler should give you 9 to 11 solid years. Badly bred ones? You'll be lucky to hit 6 or 7. And the missing years aren't the peaceful golden years—they're ripped right out of the prime. Years they should've spent hiking, guarding, clowning around on your couch. Bad genetics don't just shorten life—they steal the best part of it.

Let's also not forget stamina and drive—two things written straight into DNA. A Rottweiler bred from lazy, low-drive lines might never live up to the "working dog" standard, no matter how many agility classes you throw at them. Conversely, get one bred from driven, high-energy stock, and good luck keeping up if you thought two walks a day was "plenty." You can't nurture away what's been baked into their system for centuries.

Here's the gut punch nobody wants to hear: all the training, raw food, supplements, acupuncture, and "positive vibes only" décor in the world won't undo bad breeding. You can't "love" cancer out of a bloodline. You can't essential-oil away hip dysplasia. You can't manifest healthy hearts with Pinterest quotes. The only thing that changes the game is breeders who test, track, and give a damn. And those breeders? Rare as hell.

So let's spell out what real responsibility looks like:

OFA or PennHIP scores for hips and elbows.

Echocardiograms by board-certified cardiologists—not some stethoscope once-over at the local vet.

Thyroid panels, eye exams, DNA testing. The full alphabet soup.

Do all breeders do this? Hell no. Do backyard breeders? Not a chance. Because testing costs money. It requires rejecting dogs that "look fine." It means putting the breed above your wallet. That's what separates someone preserving Rottweilers from someone cranking out puppies for cash.

And when breeders skip those steps, who pays? Not them. You. With vet bills. With heartbreak. With watching your dog limp before their fifth birthday or collapse without warning on a morning walk. The dog pays most of all, because they live in the body their breeder handed them— and no amount of love fixes faulty wiring.

Backyard breeders are the landmines of the dog world. They don't wear warning signs. They don't introduce themselves as "Hi, I'm going to sell you a genetic dumpster fire wrapped in fur." No, they come across as normal. Harmless. Nice neighbors with a pregnant female. Sweet couple on Craigslist with "purebreds" for cheap. The guy at the bar who tells you he's got puppies ready to go, "no papers, but they're the real deal." They smile, they sound trustworthy, they swear up and down that their dogs are "healthy" and "good with kids."

What you're actually buying is a biological question mark on four legs.

Here's the truth: these people aren't thinking about bloodlines, genetic diversity, or long-term stability of the breed. They're thinking about cash. Rent money. Beer money. Vacation money. If the dog can hump, the dog can reproduce. That's the whole business model. Never mind if the parents are riddled with hip dysplasia, carrying faulty heart valves, or have a track record of chewing through the neighborhood kids. Honesty doesn't sell puppies. Puppies sell puppies.

And the lies? Oh, they've got a script. "The parents are healthy." Translation: no vet has ever actually looked at them beyond a rabies shot. "We don't believe in testing." Translation: we don't want to spend the money because vet bills eat into profits. "Farm-raised." Translation: they live outside knee-deep in shit and nobody's keeping track of who bred with whom. "We just love the breed." Translation: we just love the money the breed brings in.

Every one of those lines belongs on what I like to call **Backyard Breeder Bingo.** You can play along at home. Here's how it works:

Backyard Breeder Bingo Card (Red Flags You'll Hear Almost Word-for-Word)

- "No papers, but the parents are purebred."

- "We gave the shots ourselves."
- "The vet says they're healthy!" (which means a once-over exam, nothing more).
- "Both parents are on site!" (translation: mom and dad are locked in the backyard 24/7).
- "We don't need OFA or PennHIP, they run fine."
- "Champion bloodlines" (but can't tell you what champion, where, or in what decade).
- "This is her one and only litter." (until the next one.)
- "Socialized with kids!" (translation: the neighbor's toddler stuck a finger through the fence once).
- "You can take them today, cash only."

If you're talking to someone and you mentally tick off three of these in a row, congratulations—you just hit bingo. Only instead of a toaster oven or a vacation package, you win a Rottweiler with bad hips, unstable temperament, and a vet bill that could buy you a used car.

The worst part? Every dollar you hand one of these jokers is a vote for them to keep doing it. Every puppy sold keeps the cycle spinning. More dogs bred without testing. More families set up for heartbreak. More Rottweilers dumped into rescues at 12 to 24 months old when the cute puppy turns into a full-grown tank with a hair-trigger. And who pays the ultimate price? Not the breeder. The dog. Always the dog.

Want an example? Shelters are full of them. Meet the eighteen-month-old male Rottie, dumped because he "got aggressive." Translation: he had crap genetics, never got socialized, and when his suspicion bloomed into defensiveness, the owners had no idea how to handle it. Or the three-year-old female with hip dysplasia so bad she can't walk around the block without limping, surrendered because "she's too expensive to care for." Or the five-year-old who collapses from heart failure in the foster home—bred from parents who should never have reproduced in the first place.

And here's the kicker—these aren't "rare accidents." They're predictable outcomes. When you buy from backyard breeders, you're gambling with loaded dice. Sometimes you get lucky. Sometimes you get a disaster.

And you never know until the dog you love is limping, seizing, or leaving you too soon.

Contrast this with a real breeder. A reputable one. They're not slinging puppies out of a barn. They're screening hips, elbows, and hearts. They're tracking cancer cases. They're testing thyroids, eyes, even running DNA panels when needed. They're rejecting dogs that don't pass, even if it costs them money. They're breeding with the kind of discipline that preserves a working breed instead of trashing it. And yeah—it costs more. A well-bred Rottweiler puppy isn't $500 out of the back of a truck. But that extra cost buys you odds stacked in your favor instead of against you.

So here's my advice: if you hear lines that belong on the Backyard Breeder Bingo card, walk away. Don't negotiate. Don't think, "Well, maybe if I just save one puppy…" You're not saving anything—you're fueling the problem. Every backyard breeder survives on people with good intentions and bad information. Don't be one of them.

Rottweilers deserve better. And so do you.

Here's the bottom line: when you bring a Rottweiler into your life, you're not just buying a dog—you're buying into a genetic history. You're buying the choices breeders made years before you showed up. And that reality doesn't change just because you really, really want your dog to be perfect.

You can train your ass off. You can take every class, read every book, hire the best trainers, feed the best food. And all of it matters—don't get me wrong. But if your Rottie's DNA is a loaded gun, you're working with a weapon that already came cocked. You can keep the safety on with training and management, but you don't get to pretend the gun isn't there.

This is why "nature versus nurture" is a bullshit phrase. It's not one against the other. It's not a coin toss. It's a cocktail, and both ingredients are always in the glass. Genetics give you the blueprint. Environment builds the house. If the blueprint was garbage to begin with, you can build the hell out of it, decorate it, hang inspirational quotes on the wall, and the foundation will still crack. That's how it works.

And here's the brutal truth: most of the heartbreak stories you hear about Rottweilers—the aggressive rescues, the crippled three-year-olds, the ones who dropped dead from heart failure before their prime—they don't come from families who didn't care. They come from families who started with a loaded deck and never knew it until it was too late.

That's why your responsibility starts long before the puppy is even in your house. It starts with who you buy from. It starts with what questions you ask. It starts with whether you're willing to walk away from the "good deal" on the internet because you know damn well good genetics aren't sold like used lawnmowers on Craigslist.

You want to stack the odds in your favor? Here's what you do:

You demand proof of health testing. Not just "my vet says they're fine." Actual OFA or PennHIP certifications. Actual cardiac clearances. Paperwork, not promises.

You ask about temperament testing. Not just "the parents are sweet." Actual working titles, evaluations, or assessments that show stability.

You look at longevity in the line. Are dogs living into double digits, or are they dropping at six? That matters.

And if the breeder gives you excuses instead of answers? You walk. Period.

This isn't about being picky. This isn't about being elitist. It's about respect—for yourself, for the breed, and for the dog you're going to spend the next decade with. Because once you bring that Rottweiler home, you're locked in. There are no do-overs when a 120-pound dog with sketchy nerves decides your neighbor is a threat. There's no reset button when your dog collapses on the floor at five years old because nobody tested for SAS. You'll live with the fallout— or more accurately, your dog will.

And let's be real: Rottweilers deserve better than being treated like discount guard dogs. They deserve better than being churned out by people who think "farm raised" is a badge of honor. They deserve better than to spend their short lives sick, unstable, or abandoned because someone didn't do their homework.

So yeah, genetics matter. They matter more than the Instagram-ready puppy pictures. They matter more than the "great deal" on a litter out of somebody's backyard.

They matter more than your ego telling you "I can fix anything with training." Genetics decide the foundation. And once you accept that, you're in a position to do right by the breed.

The choice is yours: do you want to spend ten years with a stable, healthy partner who will be your shadow, your protector, your best damn friend? Or do you want to roll the dice with a backyard gamble that could cost you money, sanity, and the dog's life?

That's the reality of Rottweilers. Not the sugar-coated version. Not the fairytale. The truth.

And if you're still here, still nodding, still willing to do the work and ask the hard questions? Then congratulations—you've already proven you're the kind of human this breed actually deserves.

CHAPTER FOUR: ARE YOU WORTHY?

Don't Buy the Dog You Can't Live With

So, you've made it this far. You've read about genetics, you've nodded along, maybe even muttered a few curse words about backyard breeders. You're still here, which means you haven't slammed the book shut and gone Googling "low-maintenance dogs that don't drool." Good. But now comes the question that makes or breaks most people: are you actually the right kind of human for a Rottweiler?

Because here's the thing—owning a Rottie isn't about whether you *like* the breed. Everybody likes the breed. They're big, they're beautiful, they've got that smug head-turn that says "I could break you in half, but I choose not to." Liking them is the easy part. Living with them is the hard part.

Rottweilers were built to work. And not "help you fold laundry" kind of work. Real work. Hard, sustained, grind-it-out work. They drove cattle for miles, pulled carts heavy enough to break lesser dogs, guarded entire properties with a mix of vigilance and brawn. These dogs are working-class athletes wearing a tuxedo, and if you think they're going to be satisfied snoozing on the couch all day while you scroll TikTok, you've got another thing coming.

So picture your daily routine. Be honest. Do you wake up groggy, down two cups of coffee, commute an hour to work, sit on your ass at a desk all day, drive home, order DoorDash, and collapse into Netflix until bedtime? If that's your life, your Rottweiler will destroy you. Not because they're "bad dogs," but because that routine is poison to a working breed. You'll have a 100-pound tank with a full battery and no outlet, staring at you like, "Really? This is what we're doing? Sit? Again?"

The active owner, though—that's a different story. If you're a hiker, runner, camper, or just someone who actually enjoys moving your body, a Rottie can slot into that lifestyle beautifully. They'll match your endurance and then demand more. Hike for three hours? They'll still be bouncing around when you get back to the car. Go running every morning? Congratulations, you now have a training partner who doesn't quit. But here's the catch: even "active" owners underestimate how relentless the demand really is.

Weekend warrior types are the worst. Sedentary all week, then two monster hikes on Saturday and Sunday, followed by five days of inertia. A Rottie doesn't reset like your Fitbit. They don't work on weekly averages. They need daily, structured engagement. Miss too many days and you'll have chaos on four legs.

And don't get me started on the "but I have a yard" excuse. Every lazy owner whips that one out like it's their golden ticket. "Oh, he'll be fine, we've got two acres!" Wrong. A yard is a toilet, not a gym. I've seen Rottweilers with ranch-sized backyards who still went stir-crazy because all they did was pace the fence line like prisoners in solitary. To them, your yard is just wasted potential unless you're out there with them, turning it into something structured— training, games, tracking, weight pulls. Without you, it's just grass they shit on.

Dog parks? Don't even. That's not exercise, that's a lawsuit factory. Rottweilers don't belong in the chaos pit of a dozen untrained dogs with clueless owners scrolling Instagram while their doodle mounts everything that moves. All it takes is one insecure Rottie deciding another dog's nonsense is unacceptable, and congratulations—you're the headline in tomorrow's neighborhood Facebook group.

Lazy owners are the kiss of death here. A Rottweiler in the hands of someone who values convenience over commitment is a recipe for disaster. These are the homes where you see chewed drywall, shredded couches, destroyed shoes, and an animal with eyes blazing like, "Why the hell aren't you giving me a job?" That isn't a behavioral quirk. That's a dog telling you point-blank: "Your lifestyle doesn't fit me."

And unlike some breeds who'll tolerate that mismatch, Rottweilers don't shrink to fit. They explode.

Exercise. Training. Time. The holy trinity of Rottweiler ownership—and the three things most people underestimate, skip, or flat-out suck at. You can have the biggest heart, the best intentions, the cutest Instagram handle reserved for your future puppy, but if you drop the ball on these three, your Rottie will eat you alive. Sometimes literally.

Let's start with exercise, because everyone thinks they know what that means. "Oh, I'll walk him around the block twice a day!" That's not exercise. That's maintenance. That's the equivalent of you shuffling to the fridge and back and calling it cardio. A Rottweiler was bred to haul carts and push cattle for miles. They need output—sustained, focused, demanding output.

What does that look like? Not laps around the yard. Not ten minutes chasing a ball. Real work. Tracking drills. Obedience sessions laced into long walks. Structured tug-of-war that drains both their muscles and their mind. Weight pulls. Hiking with a backpack strapped on. Obstacle work. Hell, even having them drag a tire around the yard is better than letting them stew in boredom. The key word is structured. Left to their own devices, they don't exercise— they invent. And what they invent is rarely something you're going to appreciate.

Skip a few days and you'll see it: the restless pacing, the whining, the "bad ideas." A bored Rottweiler starts looking around your house for inspiration. Your drywall? Canvas. Your couch? Buffet. Your laundry basket? Shredding project. They're not being "naughty." They're being underemployed. You left a freight train idling with nowhere to go, and it decided to plow through your living room.

Now layer in training. If exercise is about draining the body, training is about taming the brain. And make no mistake— Rottweilers aren't "kinda smart." They're diabolically smart. The kind of smart that notices you let them slide once, and files it away forever. "Oh, so sometimes I can jump on the couch. Sometimes pulling on the leash doesn't matter. Sometimes growling at strangers gets a laugh instead of a correction. Got it. Rules are negotiable."

And once they learn rules are negotiable? They negotiate. Constantly. With leverage. Imagine playing poker every day with someone who knows all your tells and cheats just enough to win, and you're close to the Rottie experience.

Training isn't six weeks of puppy class and a certificate for your fridge. Training is daily. Lifelong. Woven into every interaction. Feeding time? Training opportunity. Opening doors? Training opportunity. That moment when the UPS guy so much as sneezes within a mile of your house and your Rottie launches into DEFCON 1 mode? Big training opportunity. You don't clock in and out as a handler. You either live the role, or you drown under it.

Here's the truth bomb no one likes admitting: Rottweilers expose every weakness you have. If you're inconsistent, they'll exploit it. If you're passive, they'll steamroll you. If you've got a short fuse, they'll meet your anger with teeth. They're mirrors with muscle, reflecting everything you do right—and everything you screw up. That's not poetic, that's survival.

And then there's time. The one resource nobody thinks about until they're tapped out. Training and exercise don't happen in "found moments." They happen every damn day, for the next decade. Most Rottweilers need a bare minimum of two hours of structured, focused engagement daily. Not belly rubs. Not lazy couch cuddles while you binge Netflix. I mean sweat-on-your-brow, brain-engaged work. Two hours. Minimum.

Think about that. Two hours a day, every day, for the next ten years. Rain, snow, exhaustion, family drama, whatever. Can you deliver? Because your Rottie won't take rain checks. Skip their time, and they'll remind you. Loudly. Destructively.

Time isn't just hours, though. It's attention. Rottweilers don't sit quietly in the background waiting for your calendar to clear. They're Velcro dogs. They want to know what you're doing, where you're going, and why the hell you closed the bathroom door without them. Ignore that need, and you don't just get a lonely dog—you get an anxious, frustrated, destructive monster with separation anxiety so bad it could win awards.

This is where most dreamers crumble. They picture a noble guardian lying stoically at their feet until danger arrives.

What they actually get is a drooling, farting, 100-pound toddler who needs jobs, rules, and your time every single day. When the reality doesn't match the dream, the dog pays the price—dumped in a yard, locked in a crate, or surrendered to rescue with the label "too much to handle."

So here's the blunt truth: if you don't have the time, don't get a Rottie. If you "sort of" have the time, don't get a Rottie. If you think you'll magically make time later, don't get a Rottie. This isn't a part-time pet. It's a full-time lifestyle.

With a Rottweiler, the question isn't "how much time will they take?" The question is: "Can you build your life around them?" Because if you can't, they'll let you know. And trust me—you won't like how they say it.

Now, let's talk money. You think it's just kibble and a couple vet visits? Think again. Owning a Rottweiler isn't just an emotional commitment—it's a financial one that will gut-punch your budget every year you've got them.

The fantasy is simple: throw them some food, a few toys, an annual rabies shot, and you're set. Reality is brutal: Rottweilers eat like linebackers, need medical care like pro athletes, and destroy things like frat boys on spring break. If you're not prepared to funnel thousands of dollars into your dog over the next decade, you're not prepared—period.

Food alone will cost you. A healthy adult Rottie can put away 4–6 cups of high-quality food a day. Not bargain-bin kibble from the grocery store—real food. Grain-free formulas, balanced raw diets, or premium kibble that doesn't read like a science experiment on the label. That's hundreds of dollars a month. Skip the good stuff, and you'll pay for it later with gut issues, skin problems, and a coat that looks like it was dragged through a fryer. Cheap food equals expensive vet bills. End of story.

Then there are the vet bills themselves. Sure, routine stuff—vaccines, flea/tick, check-ups—already runs more than your average small dog. But it's the surprise bills that bankrupt people. Foreign body surgery because your Rottie swallowed a sock? $4,000. ACL repair after they launched themselves off your deck like a stuntman? $6,000–$8,000. Chemotherapy for osteosarcoma? Easily five figures, with no guarantee of more than months.

And that's before we even mention breed-specific landmines like hip dysplasia or heart disease. The truth? If you don't have an "Oh Shit" fund set aside, you'll eventually be staring down a vet estimate that makes you feel like you've just been handed a mortgage payment for a house you don't even live in. Some people pay it. Some people can't. And some people take the quiet, shameful route of euthanasia because they weren't ready for the costs. If that last one makes you squirm, good. It should.

Training is another bill most owners pretend doesn't exist. Spoiler: it does. Whether it's group classes, private trainers, or sport clubs, you will pay in both dollars and time. Think of it as tuition. Pay it now, and you'll have a stable, trained dog. Skip it, and you'll pay later—in chaos, destruction, or lawsuits. A single bite incident can cost more than every trainer you'll ever hire. Training isn't a luxury for this breed. It's a line item in your budget.

And then there's the destruction fund. If you don't crate train properly, your Rottweiler will absolutely redecorate your house. And by "redecorate," I mean they'll chew your baseboards into mulch, turn your couch into confetti, and turn your drywall into Swiss cheese. Drywall repairs. New shoes. Replacement remotes. Furniture you swore would last ten years. Kiss it goodbye. You can either invest in crates, chew toys, and training—or pay the price in Home Depot receipts.

Insurance? Oh yeah, add that too. Plenty of homeowner policies either ban Rottweilers outright or jack your premium because of the "dangerous breed" label. Renters? Good luck finding a landlord who's cool with a 120-pound liability on four legs. You may end up paying higher deposits, restricted leases, or flat-out being denied housing. That's not fair—but it's real.

And let's not forget time as currency. Time is money, and Rottweilers demand both. Two hours of structured engagement daily, for a decade. Multiple vet visits when health issues pop up. Hours of training sessions, day after day. That's time you won't spend on Netflix, hobbies, or spontaneous weekends away. If you think you can just "fit them in," you're lying to yourself. With a Rottweiler, you don't fit them in—you build your life around them.

Here's the punchline: the true cost of a Rottweiler isn't just food or vet bills. It's lifestyle. It's time you'll never get back, money you'll never see again, and sacrifices you'll have to make whether you planned for them or not. For the right person, it's worth it a thousand times over. For the unprepared? It's ruin.

And then there are the people who flat-out shouldn't own a Rottweiler. That's not elitist—it's reality.

The first type is the absentee crowd, the ones who work twelve-hour shifts, travel every other week, or proudly admit they're "never home much." For them, a Rottweiler is a death sentence wrapped in fur. This breed doesn't sit quietly in a corner waiting for you to stroll back into their life. They unravel. They become frantic, destructive, or hollowed-out shells of themselves. And no, a dog walker three times a week won't cut it. No, toys won't substitute for you. A Rottweiler doesn't need background noise—they need their person. If you can't be present, they will suffer, and it's not a fair trade.

Then there are the inconsistent owners—the "sometimes" people. Sometimes the dog's allowed on the couch, sometimes not. Sometimes growling at a stranger is hilarious, sometimes it's punished. Sometimes pulling on the leash is ignored, sometimes it sparks a tug-of-war. Dogs don't thrive on "sometimes." They thrive on rules, consistency, predictability. And when you destabilize a Rottweiler with half-assed leadership, you don't just confuse them—you create insecurity. In this breed, insecurity isn't just sad, it's dangerous. A confused Rottweiler doesn't guess softly. They draw their own rules, and those rules usually come with teeth.

And finally, there's the status-symbol crowd—the worst offenders of all. You've seen them: sleeveless guy strutting down the sidewalk with a chain collar and a Rottweiler at his side, puffing up his chest like he's starring in a low-budget action movie. They don't see a partner; they see a prop. They brag about how "badass" their dog looks, they laugh when it growls at strangers, they think dominance is the same thing as training. Owning a Rottweiler for ego points is like buying a loaded gun because you think it matches your outfit. It's not just stupid, it's dangerous—for the dog, for the owner, and for every single person unlucky enough to cross paths with them.

The sad part is, these are the owners who make the headlines when their untrained, unstable dog finally explodes. And every time it happens, the whole breed takes the hit. More bans. More restrictions. More stigma. All because someone wanted a trophy and ended up with a ticking time bomb. Meanwhile, the dog—the innocent one in all this—is the one who pays the ultimate price.

That's the bottom line: not everyone deserves this breed. If you're absent, inconsistent, or just looking for a four-legged status symbol, you're not just a bad fit—you're a liability. And the worst part? You won't be the one paying the real bill. The Rottweiler will.

And even if you *are* the right kind of person, willing to show up, stay consistent, and treat this dog like the full-time commitment they are—there's still one more wall waiting to hit you square in the face. It's not about lifestyle. It's not about discipline. It's about your wallet. Because loving a Rottweiler isn't enough if you can't afford one. If you thought the commitment was heavy, wait until you see the bill.

CHAPTER FIVE:

THE REAL PRICE OF A ROTTWEILER (A WALLET CHECK)

The financial gut punch starts before your Rottweiler even sets paw in your house. The initial buy-in is where most people stumble, either because they fall for the bargain-bin puppy or because they don't realize just how fast "starter gear" snowballs into a receipt the length of your arm.

A well-bred puppy from a responsible breeder will run you anywhere from two to three grand, and that's not price-gouging—it's what it costs to support health testing, quality care, and a breeder who actually gives a damn about where their dogs end up. A "cheap" Rottweiler from Craigslist or the neighbor's "oops litter" might look like a steal at a few hundred bucks, but you'll pay it back tenfold in vet bills, training nightmares, and heartache. Rescue fees are lower—usually three to six hundred dollars—but don't kid yourself: the real expenses begin the minute that dog walks through your door, no matter where it came from.

And then there's the starter kit, which is less "kit" and more "financial black hole." Crates, gates, bowls, collars, leashes, toys, training treats, and a bed your Rottie will probably explode like a confetti bomb within a week. Toss in puppy vaccines, spay or neuter if it's not already done, microchipping, and the inevitable "oh God, what did you just swallow?" emergency vet visit, and you're easily two grand deep before you've even finished house-training.

This is the moment where most people realize they haven't just bought a dog—they've bought a lifestyle. That breeder fee or adoption charge was just the down payment. The real mortgage on a Rottweiler comes monthly, and it never stops until the day they're gone.

The baseline costs pile up quickly, and they don't politely spread themselves out on your calendar. They hit like waves, constant and relentless. Food alone will drain a grand or two a year if you're feeding quality kibble or raw. And before you try to get clever—no, you can't skimp. A hundred-pound dog running on bargain food is like fueling a Ferrari with lawnmower gas: it'll run, sure, but it'll sputter, cough, and eventually break down in ways that cost you far more than the money you "saved."

Vet care is another unavoidable line item. Annual exams, vaccines, flea and tick prevention, heartworm meds—you're already at five hundred to a grand a year if nothing goes wrong. That's the baseline, and if you've read the chapters on genetics, you already know something will eventually go wrong. Add insurance premiums, which are higher thanks to the "dangerous breed" stigma, and you're suddenly shelling out the equivalent of a small car payment every single month just to keep your dog healthy and covered.

Training? Non-negotiable. Whether it's obedience classes, private lessons, or sport clubs, you'll drop another grand or two every year, and that's if you're disciplined about doing the bulk of the work yourself. Pretend you don't need it, and you'll pay for it later—when your untrained Rottie decides to "problem-solve" by flattening your neighbor's schnauzer.

And then there's the stuff nobody budgets for but everybody buys anyway: toys, leashes, harnesses, chew bones, indestructible balls that mysteriously self-destruct in thirty seconds. Rottweilers don't just play with toys, they stress test them. Every single one. That $30 tug toy you thought would last a year? Gone in a week. Meanwhile, the squeaky thing you hate will survive nuclear war.

Stack it all together and the yearly baseline easily cracks four or five grand. That's before surprises. That's before emergencies. That's before the couch your Rottweiler "remodeled" or the ACL surgery that comes out of nowhere. Four or five grand, every single year, just to tread water.

Here's where things get fun—if by "fun" you mean the kind of financial ambush that makes you stare at your bank account like it just personally betrayed you. Surprise costs are the silent killers of Rottweiler ownership. They don't show up neatly on a budget spreadsheet. They kick down your door at two in the morning, and suddenly you're swiping your credit card with sweaty hands while your dog gives you the big sad eyes from an emergency vet gurney.

The most common ambush is surgery. Rottweilers are walking appetites with zero discretion, which means at some point, you'll probably be staring at an X-ray of a stomach full of socks, rocks, or half a chew toy. The vet will look at you with that "we both know what comes next" expression, and you'll be signing off on a three to five grand foreign-body removal. If you're really unlucky and it's a blown ACL, brace yourself for a five-to-eight-thousand-dollar repair. Multiply that by two, because yes, dogs often tear both.

And let's not pretend chronic illness doesn't exist. Allergies that turn into endless vet visits, thyroid issues that require daily medication, skin conditions that never really go away—each one is death by a thousand cuts to your wallet. Add in breed-specific landmines like hip dysplasia, heart disease, or osteosarcoma, and suddenly you're not just budgeting for a dog—you're budgeting for a second mortgage.

Then there's the property damage, which comes standard with bored Rottweilers and inexperienced owners. Drywall is apparently delicious. Couch cushions? Better than any chew toy. Remote controls? Gone in one bite. I've seen dogs rip through baseboards, chew through door frames, and redecorate entire living rooms in the time it takes to run a quick errand. Repairs can run into the hundreds or even thousands, depending on how creative your dog is. And trust me—they're creative.

Let's not forget the hidden costs of living with a "restricted breed." Insurance companies hike your rates, some landlords won't even let you in the building, and boarding facilities either refuse outright or charge extra for "large guardian breeds." Want to travel? Be ready to drop thousands on specialized boarding or pet sitters, because Aunt Linda isn't going to watch your 120-pound Rottie after the last time he ate her throw pillows.

These aren't "maybe" expenses. They're inevitabilities. At some point in your Rottweiler's life, you will get hit with at least one major emergency bill, several smaller chronic ones, and a steady trickle of destruction repair. If you can absorb those hits without spiraling into resentment or financial ruin, great—you're in the right lane. If the very idea makes your stomach flip, then here's your reality check: you're not ready for this breed.

So let's tally this up, shall we? Because while it's easy to talk about surprise vet bills and chewed-up furniture in isolation, the real gut punch is when you add it all together and see the lifetime cost of owning a Rottweiler staring back at you like a bad credit card statement.

The baseline, if you're disciplined and lucky, is somewhere in the neighborhood of **$20,000 to $40,000** over the course of a typical Rottie's life. That's food, routine vet care, training, supplies, and the odd chewed-up couch cushion. Manageable if you budget, plan, and accept that this dog eats more than most teenagers.

But that's the *best case*. Add in even one or two big emergencies, a chronic health issue, or an owner who gets ambitious with dog sports, and suddenly you're staring down **$60,000, $70,000, even $80,000+** over ten years. That's not hyperbole—it's math. ACL surgeries, cancer treatments, advanced diagnostics, specialized trainers, premium food—it all stacks up faster than you think.

Here's the kicker: most people never run those numbers before they bring home a puppy. They picture the dog itself as the purchase, when really, the purchase is the *lifestyle*—a lifestyle that comes with a recurring bill you don't get to opt out of. With a Rottweiler, the meter is always running, and unlike your Netflix subscription, you can't just cancel when it gets inconvenient.

So what's the lifetime price of a Rottie? Here's the blunt answer: it's whatever you've got, and sometimes more. They'll take your money, your time, your weekends, your patience. And if you're the right kind of person, you'll give it all without hesitation. Because in return, you get something money can't really buy: a partner who will guard your life, burrow into your heart, and love you with a loyalty so fierce it makes the spreadsheets worth it.

But don't kid yourself—it's not free, and it's not cheap. Every dollar you spend is an investment in keeping your Rottweiler healthy, sane, and safe. If that sounds like too much, do both yourself and the breed a favor: step away. If it sounds worth it—even knowing the price—then congratulations. You're one of the few who actually gets it.

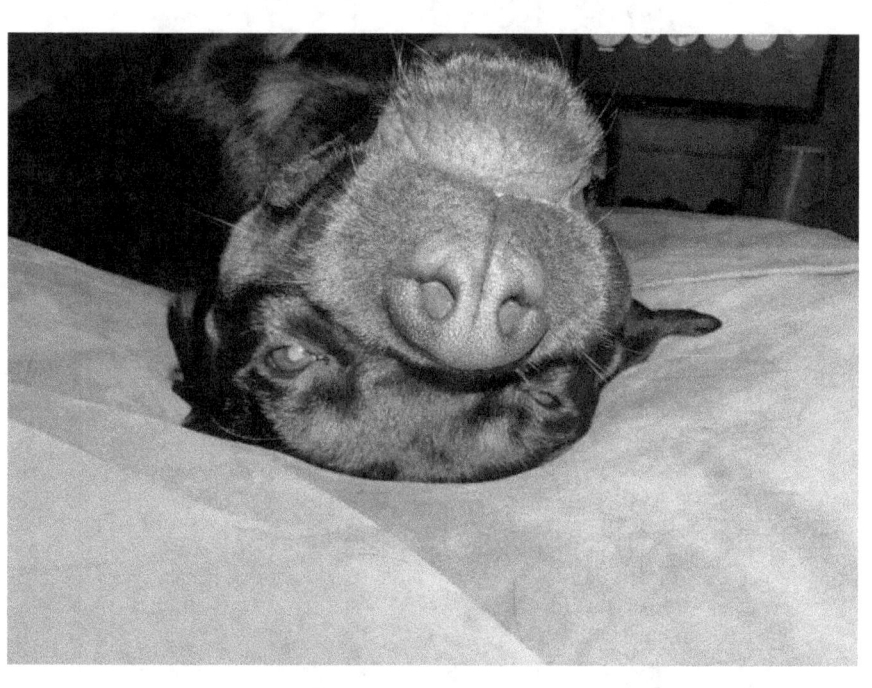

CHAPTER SIX:

GETTING READY FOR YOUR ROTTWEILER PUPPY

The biggest lie people tell themselves when getting a dog—especially a Rottweiler—is that the hard part comes later. That it'll start when the puppy begins chewing furniture, or when the housebreaking hits a snag, or maybe when they realize the dog needs more than just a backyard and a pat on the head to stay sane. But that's not the hard part. That's just the part that makes noise.

The hard part comes before the puppy ever sets foot in your house. It starts the moment you decide where that dog is coming from. Most people screw it up before they even know they're in danger. They think they're just buying a puppy. What they're actually doing is setting the tone for the next decade of their life. And they're either building the foundation for something great... or signing up for heartbreak with a bark.

You'd be amazed how many people think they've scored a smart deal because they "knew a guy," or found a listing on Craigslist that said "purebred, no papers," or spotted a hand-painted sign off the highway that read ROTTWEILER PUPS: CASH ONLY. The puppy was cute, the seller was friendly, the price was low—and they convinced themselves it was just good luck.

It never is.

This is why shelters are full. It's why trainers are booked six months out and why some vets break the news with a sigh and an apology. It's not just bad luck. It's predictable failure. And it almost always starts with a garbage breeder.

This isn't just about doing the "ethical" thing. This is about odds. When you get a poorly bred puppy, you're gambling—with your time, your money, and your emotional bandwidth. Bad genetics and lazy pairings don't always explode on day one, but they will show up eventually: in medical bills, unpredictable behavior, aggression, heartbreak, or worse.

Real breeders don't just make puppies. They build dogs. And they do it with surgical precision. They study pedigrees. They test hips, elbows, hearts, and DNA like they're preparing to launch a new species into space. They can tell you which grandparent had soft rears, which uncle couldn't pass a temperament test, and which dam throws stable, confident pups. They're not "into dogs." They're obsessed. And that's exactly who you want.

They won't just take your money and wave goodbye. They'll interview you harder than any job application you've ever filled out. They'll ask where you live, what kind of fencing you have, whether your whole household is on board, what you plan to do if the dog develops reactivity, how many hours you're away from home, and what you'll do when things get hard. They're not being difficult. They're weeding out future regrets.

And if you're not a fit, they'll tell you. Politely, directly, without apology. Unethical breeders? They never say no. They never ask questions. They just smile, take your cash, and send you off with a wagging tail and a ticking time bomb.

When you get your dog from that kind of operation—the no-papers, no-testing, "we've never had problems" operation—you're not getting a clean slate. You're getting a backlog of mistakes you'll spend years trying to undo. These are the dogs with fragile bodies and unstable nerves. The ones who chew through drywall and snap under pressure. The ones who can't handle stress, fear strangers, explode during adolescence, and end up either muzzled, medicated, or dead before their third birthday.

A responsible breeder, on the other hand, gives you more than a puppy. They give you a foundation: a dog with sound structure, proven temperament, and support on the other end of the phone when your puppy starts growling at the crate or eating drywall. Their dogs aren't accidents.

They're legacies—bred with purpose, pressure-tested, and thoughtfully placed.

Here's how you'll know you've found the right one: they won't try to sell you. They won't push you to commit. They'll be relieved if you take time to think, and they'll talk more about structure and temperament than price. You'll leave the conversation feeling like you just signed up for something serious. Because you did.

You'll also know when you've found the wrong one. The cash-only seller who promises "rare colors," "XXL bloodlines," or puppies available right now with no waitlist, no contract, and no paperwork? That's a walking red flag. If they get defensive when you ask about health testing, if they don't have both parents on site—or worse, if they won't let you visit until pickup day—run.

Because the dog you bring home from that person won't come with just bad papers. It'll come with bad wiring. And when that wiring sparks six months down the line and your Rottweiler starts showing signs of reactivity, fear aggression, or medical fragility, there won't be a support system. There'll be silence. Or worse, denial.

And let's clear this up right now: "rare" Rottweiler colors aren't rare. They're wrong. Merle, blue, white, panda— those aren't unicorns. They're red flags painted like rainbows. That's not a special bloodline. That's a health hazard with branding.

If the price tag on a well-bred puppy feels steep to you— two, three, maybe even four grand—consider it the first and cheapest part of Rottweiler ownership. Because if that sounds like too much? You're absolutely not ready for what comes next. Vet bills, training, insurance, food, gear, injuries. That upfront price isn't the cost. It's just the entry fee.

And for anyone wondering about the timeline? Start early. You don't "find" a breeder in a weekend. You research. You stalk websites. You email. You wait. You interview, and you get interviewed. And when the litter finally lands, you wait again—eight weeks minimum before that pup sets foot in your house.

That time matters. Use it.

Because the decisions you make now—the breeder you choose, the questions you ask, the standards you enforce—will shape everything that comes next. The training. The temperament. The trust. The freedom. The future.

Buy wisely. Ask hard questions. And if something feels off, walk away.

No puppy is cute enough to make up for a decade of regret.

Assuming you passed that test and found someone legit, congrats—you're halfway to chaos. Now you have to survive where that chaos lands: your house.

People love to romanticize the day they bring their puppy home. They post the car ride photos with the little potato tucked into a blanket, ears flopped over, big innocent eyes staring out the window like they're already dreaming about becoming a therapy dog.

What those pictures don't show is the carnage waiting back at the house. The sock funerals. The shredded phone chargers. The drywall that didn't survive the first week. Because here's the part every Pinterest puppy checklist conveniently forgets to mention:

Your home is not ready.

No, seriously. Not even close.

You are not preparing your house for a baby. You are preparing it for a land shark with zero self-control, no moral compass, and an unhealthy interest in electrical wiring. This is not an exaggeration. It's damage control—before the damage happens.

If it's on the floor, it belongs to the puppy. If it dangles off a table, it's fair game. If it smells weird, it's already in their mouth. Your Rottweiler puppy will come in like a tiny wrecking ball wrapped in fur, and you will lose things. Belongings. Sleep. Dignity.

Start with the obvious: anything valuable, sentimental, or chewable needs to disappear. Cords? Hide them or lose Wi-Fi mid-call. Trash cans? Lock them down or prepare for a buffet of horrors. Shoes? Don't even try to "just move them out of reach." There is no "out of reach."

This dog isn't stupid. They're curious, stubborn, and surprisingly athletic.

Pillows? Ripped. Laundry? Swallowed. Books? Gone. Remote controls? Now a chew toy.

Your "open floor plan"? That's a battlefield. Get baby gates. Not one—several. Create zones. Defend doorways. Block off anything you can't handle being ruined, because your puppy has no boundaries and even less respect for yours.

And then there's the crate.

If you think crates are "mean," you're not ready for this breed. Crates aren't punishment. They're structure. They're the difference between a controlled environment and waking up at 3 a.m. to the sound of drywall being murdered. A crate is how you keep your puppy—and your house—alive.

Buy a crate big enough for a full-grown Rottweiler, with a divider to adjust as they grow. Place it where the puppy can rest without being isolated. Use it often. Rotate between supervised play and crate time like it's religion. You can't supervise a puppy 24/7, and pretending otherwise is how you end up paying for surgery or drywall repairs by week two.

And don't stop at crates. You'll need an ex-pen or two. These aren't luxuries. They're buffer zones between the chaos and your sanity. You need places to park your dog when you're not actively training, playing, or watching like a hawk. If they're loose in the house, someone better be watching—and no, "I was in the same room" doesn't count. That's how the couch dies.

Here's a universal rule: if you can't give 100% supervision, they go in the crate or pen. No exceptions.

Houseplants? Potentially toxic. Cabinets? Install latches. Toiletries? Locked up. Cleaning supplies? Moved higher. That laundry basket full of socks? That's a $4,000 vet bill waiting to happen. Rottweiler puppies don't "outgrow" chaos. They graduate into larger chaos with better reach.

Don't trust your puppy. Ever. They will find the thing you forgot to move. They will chew it. They will swallow part of it. And when they're vomiting glitter or sneezing out part of a sandal, you'll realize you weren't as prepared as you thought.

This is not about paranoia. This is about math. Odds are, if something can go wrong—it will. So you build a system that limits risk and sets your puppy up to succeed.

And here's the part no one admits: some stuff is going to get destroyed anyway. That's part of the deal. You're not just raising a dog—you're raising a demolition crew with separation anxiety. Accept the loss. Save what you can. Plan like the rest is already gone.

The goal here isn't perfection. It's damage control.

Because the more you control the environment, the less time you spend yelling "NO" at a puppy that doesn't speak English. You don't want to be reactive. You want to be five steps ahead, with a leash in one hand, treats in the other, and your AirPods safely locked in a drawer where they can't become chew toys.

If you do this right, you'll survive the early chaos with only minor injuries—financial, emotional, and probably literal.

If you don't?

Well. Let's just say drywall isn't covered by pet insurance.

And the moment you think you've got it under control— boom. The dog comes home.

The moment you carry your Rottweiler puppy through the front door, everything changes. For you. For your house. For your nervous system. The puppy? They're just vibing— sniffing things, chewing things, peeing on things—with the energy of a toddler on espresso.

You, on the other hand, are about to question every life choice you've made in the last six months.

Everyone talks about how exciting it is to bring a new puppy home. What they don't mention is that it feels less like a family milestone and more like hosting a wild animal in your living room—with no instructions, no off switch, and no respect for your furniture.

The first 48 hours are not magical. They're not peaceful. They are not the start of a Disney montage.

They are loud. Messy. Overwhelming. And if you're not ready for that, they'll break you.

Let's walk through what this actually looks like.

You pick up the puppy. Maybe they whine a little in the car. Maybe they throw up. Maybe they fall asleep in your lap and trick you into thinking this is going to be easy.

Spoiler: it's not.

You get home. You set them down. You take a deep breath and think, This is it—our new beginning.

And in less than five minutes, they've peed on the tile, found a loose sock, and are chewing the leg of the coffee table like it personally insulted them.

This is not misbehavior. This is not rebellion. This is what untrained, overstimulated baby dogs do. They don't know the rules. You haven't taught them anything yet. The chaos is not a sign of failure—it's the default setting.

Now's the moment when your prep work starts to pay off. Or doesn't.

If you've got gates up, a crate ready, pens set, shoes hidden, and trash locked down—great. You're ahead of the game. If you've got none of that? Well, I hope your vet takes payment plans.

The first day is about containment, observation, and structure. This is not the time to give them free reign "to explore." You're not raising a child at Montessori. You're managing a landmine with teeth.

Crate training begins immediately. Not "once they're settled." Not "after they nap on my chest." Now. Day one. The longer you wait, the louder the protest will be when you finally close that crate door.

And oh, they'll protest.

They'll scream. They'll cry. They'll bark, howl, whimper, and rattle the bars like a jail scene in a bad movie. You'll sit on the floor, guilt flooding your chest, convincing yourself that maybe just one night in bed with you won't hurt.

It will.

Because the moment you cave, you've taught them that throwing a tantrum works. And now they'll do it every single time.

This isn't cruelty. This is survival training—for both of you. The crate is a sleep zone. A safe space. A place to decompress, not a punishment box. You don't wait for them to "accept it." You make it a non-negotiable part of the routine from minute one.

Speaking of routines—create one.

Feeding schedule. Water schedule. Potty breaks every 30 to 60 minutes, including:

- Right after naps
- Right after eating
- Right after playing
- Right before bed

If they're awake, assume they need to pee. If they disappear for more than 30 seconds, assume they're peeing right now behind the couch.

And when the accidents happen—and they will—don't lose your mind. Don't yell. Don't scold. Don't rub their nose in it like some outdated dominance nonsense book told you. Just clean it up, make a mental note of where you failed, and adjust.

Trust me, it's your fault. Not theirs.

Oh—and don't trust quiet puppies. Quiet means sleeping or plotting. That's it. If you can't supervise with both eyes, they go in the crate or get tethered to you with a leash. Let them wander, and you'll find them under the dining table with the TV remote halfway down their throat.

Now let's talk about sleep. For them, and for you.

New puppies are jet-lagged. Emotionally, physically, and socially. They just left their litter, their mother, and everything familiar. So yeah—they'll cry at night. They'll miss the warmth and heartbeat of their siblings. They'll be confused and scared. And you'll feel like a monster for not comforting them.

You're not a monster.

You're an adult making the hard choice now to avoid the harder consequences later.

Set up the crate near your bed for the first few nights if you must—but don't take them out just because they're making noise. Take them out if they need to go, not because you feel bad. Keep it quiet, boring, and brief. No cuddles. No play. Back to bed.

One pee, one poop, one crate. That's the loop.

Will you sleep much? No. Welcome to dog ownership. You signed up for this.

The first 48 hours are about endurance. You will cry. You will doubt yourself. You will wonder if you've made a massive mistake.

That's normal.

But you'll also catch moments—small ones—where the puppy locks eyes with you, or collapses into your lap, or falls asleep with their nose under your hand, and you'll feel it: the start of something real.

Just survive the first 48.

After that, you're not out of the woods—but you're at least standing on the path.

And once the crate crying fades and the accidents slow down?

That's when the biting begins.

And it gets worse before it gets better.

Nobody tells you this part when you're dreaming about your perfect puppy curled up in a sunbeam. But it hits fast—and it hits hard.

Rottweiler puppies bite.

Not like "Oops, a gentle nibble." We're talking full-blown, Tasmanian-devil-mode, sink-their-tiny-razor-teeth-into-anything-that-moves biting. Arms, ankles, pant legs, ears, furniture, exposed toes. Nothing is sacred.

And yes, it's normal. It still sucks.

This isn't aggression. This isn't a red flag. This is your puppy learning how their mouth works. It's developmental, it's necessary—and it will make you question whether your dog is possessed.

Because it's not just the biting. It's the intensity. They latch on and commit like they're training for the canine UFC. And no, "No bite" doesn't work. Neither does yelping like a littermate. That just gets them more excited.

They're not trying to hurt you. But they absolutely will.

So now you're panicked. You tell them "no." They bite harder. You pull your hand back. They leap for your sleeve. You try to redirect. They think it's a game. And now you're locked in a battle with a twelve-pound demon who thinks your forearms are enrichment toys.

Here's your reality check: you're not stopping the biting. You're managing it.

Step one: manage the state, not just the mouth.

Nine times out of ten, your puppy isn't biting because they're mean—they're biting because they're overtired, overstimulated, or under-supervised. When they start running zoomies, growling, spinning, biting the air like they've been possessed, that's not play. That's a meltdown.

Crate. Nap. Reset.

If you keep trying to "train through it," you're just fueling the fire. Exhausted puppies act like drunk toddlers with knives. They don't need more stimulation. They need a dark room, a frozen Kong, and a goddamn nap.

Step two: stop letting them rehearse bad habits on your skin.

Your hands? Not toys. Your pants? Not tug ropes. Your kids? Definitely not fair game.

You need high-value, durable chew options ready at all times. Not squeaky plush toys that last six minutes. Not discount-store tennis balls with a chew-time death sentence. Real chews. Frozen Kongs. Rope toys. Rubber rings. Things that can take a beating.

And when your puppy bites you instead of the toy? Stop the game. Immediately. Zero drama. No yelling. No theatrics. Just end it. Into the crate or onto a leash tether away from the fun.

Fun stops when teeth land on skin. Period.

Step three: stop underestimating how much structure they need.

You think, "They just need to get it out of their system." No. What they need is fewer options. Clear limits. A routine that builds calm instead of chaos. Puppies that know what's coming next are easier to live with. Puppies that live in unstructured free-for-alls will turn into bitey, overstimulated maniacs.

Step four: build their brain.

Even young puppies can learn impulse control. Sit. Down. Touch. Place. Wait for food. Focus work. Reward calm.

Training isn't just about commands—it's about teaching the puppy how to think. Thinking dogs bite less. Thinking dogs settle faster. Thinking dogs learn to pause before launching at your kneecaps.

And finally: stop panicking.

You will get bruises. You will lose a sock or three. You will look down at your hand and see tiny teeth marks and wonder what the hell you signed up for.

You'll think, "This can't be normal."

It is.

And it gets better.

The phase ends. The teeth dull. The brain catches up. The meltdowns fade. The monster becomes manageable. Then trustworthy. Then—if you stay the course—pretty damn impressive.

But right now? Right now you're in the middle of it. And survival means outsmarting the teeth. Crating before chaos. Catching the overstimulation before it turns into a gremlin attack.

So stock the freezer. Hide your favorite hoodie. Keep your expectations realistic and your reactions boring.

Your puppy isn't broken.

They're just bitey.

And your job isn't to fix it overnight—it's to ride the wave without turning into a chew toy.

You'll get there.

Probably with some scars. But smarter, tougher, and with a dog who—eventually—knows the difference between tug time and your hand.

And when you do, you'll realize half your gear didn't survive—and the other half wasn't built for this breed.

There's a moment every Rottweiler owner has—usually sometime during week two—where they're standing in the middle of a pet store, holding three leashes they don't trust, wondering why nothing they bought is working.

That's when it hits them: they didn't buy what they actually needed.

They bought the "starter pack." The cute food bowls. The bed that looked Instagram-worthy. A few chew toys recommended by someone's blog. But they didn't buy gear built for war. And puppyhood? Is war.

So here's your post-bite-recovery reality check. You need stuff that holds up. Stuff that contains chaos. Stuff that survives spit, teeth, panic, and power. Because your Rottweiler puppy? They're not here for aesthetics. They're here to break things and test boundaries. Let's make sure you're ready.

Start with the crate. If you skipped it, fix that now. You're not just buying a nap box—you're buying a survival bunker. Big enough to fit them full-grown, but adjustable while they're small. This isn't optional. Puppies with too much freedom end up with vet bills and body counts. (RIP, couch cushion #3.)

You'll also want an ex-pen. This is your puppy's off-duty containment zone. Not a prison—more like a bite-free buffer between "I can't watch you" and "you're eating drywall again." Get a tall one. Rotties bounce higher than you think, especially when they've discovered the thrill of baseboard destruction.

Baby gates? Install them like your mental health depends on it—because it does. You need control points. You need to divide and conquer. Free-roaming puppies are not independent. They're just unsupervised.

Now leashes. You need at least three.

A short, durable leash for everyday control.

A long line for recall training and backyard play without trust.

A backup leash for your car or emergency oh-god-he-got-loose moment.

And for the love of sanity, skip the retractable leash. That's not a tool. That's a liability. If you want your dog to slingshot into traffic, sure, go ahead. Otherwise, burn it.

Collars? Fitted flat collar for ID. Harness or slip lead for training—with instruction. If you don't know how to use it, don't guess. You're not in a Fast & Furious movie. Control isn't about horsepower. It's about clarity.

Now let's talk toys.

Spoiler: you're going to waste money. That's just part of the process. But you can waste it intelligently.

Don't bother with plush, squeaky "tough" toys unless you enjoy watching $30 die in under five minutes. Your Rottweiler is a durability test lab. Get real chews—frozen Kongs, rubber bones, rope toys (supervised), and age-appropriate bones or antlers.

Pro tip: always supervise the first chew session with a new toy. Just because it says "indestructible" doesn't mean your dog got the memo.

And don't forget training treats. Not the dry biscuits that crumble into dust. You need high-value, easy-to-chew motivators. Soft stuff. Real meat. Boiled chicken. Liver. Freeze-dried chaos fuel. You'll be handing out a lot of them, especially if you plan to survive crate training, recall, leash manners, and the 400 "leave it"s you'll issue in the next month.

On the feeding front, get a slow feeder. Bloat is real. You think it's funny when they vacuum their food in 12 seconds—until you're in the emergency clinic asking, "What do you mean his stomach flipped?"

Also: poop bags. So many poop bags. One in every coat, car, drawer, and training bag. Poop scooper. Enzymatic cleaner. Wipes. And a backup plan for when they vomit something unspeakable at 2 a.m.

You'll want nail clippers or a Dremel (get your puppy used to it early), ear cleaner, and a pet thermometer (the kind you didn't know existed until your vet said, "Take their temperature.")

Bonus tip: create a "puppy file." Physical or digital—doesn't matter. Keep breeder info, vet records, vaccine dates, insurance policy, microchip registration, and trainer contacts in one place. When chaos hits—and it will—you'll be glad you're not rifling through drawers at midnight.

And yes, get a trainer. Not after things go sideways. Now. Before your puppy learns the wrong lessons. Before you create habits you'll regret. Before you're Googling "why does my dog bite children in hoodies."

Because all this gear? It helps. But it doesn't replace leadership.

You can't buy your way out of structure. You can't treat your way out of a confidence issue. You can't leash-solve a dog that never learned impulse control.

But with the right gear—and the right mindset—you can at least survive the first few months without losing your house, your sanity, or your relationship.

Buy what works. Replace what breaks. And stop thinking you'll "figure it out later."

Later's too late.

Especially when the puppy's got your AirPods in their mouth and you're realizing the "cute" collar you bought won't hold them during a panic sprint.

Learn from other people's mistakes.

Or make your own and buy twice.

Your call.

If you've made it this far—through the breeder gauntlet, the Craigslist temptations, the land-shark apocalypse, and the 2 a.m. scream-fests—you're already ahead of the curve. But survival isn't the same as success.

Now comes the part most people screw up not because they're lazy, but because they think they have time.

You don't.

The clock started the moment your puppy stepped into your house. Every hour, every outing, every new experience—your dog is collecting data. About the world. About you. About how to respond when things get weird or loud or stressful.

And if you're not the one shaping that frame of reference, guess who is?

Everything.

Every stranger. Every sound. Every movement. Every random moment where your dog had to decide whether the world was safe or dangerous, while you were busy thinking they were "too young to train."

There's no neutral with Rottweilers. They're not born blank slates. They're born calculators. Pressure readers. Pattern recognizers. They don't forget what scared them—and they don't forgive sloppy leadership.

So when someone says, "I didn't want to over-socialize because I want them to be protective," what they're actually saying is, "I don't understand the difference between confidence and reactivity."

Let's fix that.

Socialization doesn't cancel out protection. It teaches your dog what's normal. It teaches them what's none of their business. It gives them a library of "not a threat" examples so that, when something truly is a threat, they don't hesitate—they respond. Calmly. With clarity.

You don't get a reliable guardian by raising a shut-in.

And no, this isn't about tossing your puppy into chaos and hoping they swim. That's not socialization—that's flooding. That's how you create dogs that either shut down or lash out. You want measured exposure. New people, new surfaces, new sounds, new places—introduced with intent. Not all at once. Not without escape routes. Not as a test.

Watch your dog. Read the body. End on wins.

Teach them that the world makes sense—and that you're the one making sense of it for them.

At the same time, training starts now. Not later. Not "when they're old enough." Now.

You're already training them. Every single interaction is training. Every time they bite and you laugh, you're training. Every time they ignore your voice and you let it slide, you're training. Every time you ask them to come and then do nothing when they don't? Training.

Delayed training is still training. It just produces worse results.

So don't waste these early weeks. Don't pretend they're "just a baby." Rottweilers are learning machines, and if you don't give them structure, they'll build their own—with rules you won't like.

This doesn't mean military drills in your backyard at 10 weeks. It means name recognition. Coming when called. Learning that your hands feed, not flail. That pulling ends walks. That calm earns praise. That chaos earns containment.

It means boundaries, not just corrections. It means consistency, not just commands.

Hire a trainer before the problems start. Someone who understands working dogs. Someone who teaches communication, not just control. Because this breed doesn't respond to brute force—but they also don't tolerate vagueness.

You'll mess up. You'll get frustrated. You'll contradict yourself. You'll cry. Welcome to raising a Rottie. There's no straight path. But what matters is that you keep showing up. That you adjust. That you lead.

Because if you don't lead, your Rottweiler will.

And that's not a hypothetical. That's a pattern—one that ends in reactivity, resentment, and regrets you can't undo.

But if you do it right?

If you put in the work now—when it's inconvenient, exhausting, and thankless—you'll build a dog you can live with. A dog that knows how to turn on when needed and shut off when safe. A dog that holds their commands even under pressure. A dog that earns you the kind of peace no tool can replicate.

The kind of dog that makes people ask, "How the hell did you train that?"

And you'll know the answer.

Because you were there at week nine, sweating through leash drills and desensitization reps. You were the one who said no when it was hard. You were the one who saw the little things before they turned into big things.

You were the one who showed up.

That's the difference.

That's the fork in the road every Rottweiler owner hits—and most never even realize they're standing at it.

You're not just training a dog. You're raising a life that could either be your greatest success… or your biggest mistake.

What you do right now decides which one it'll be.

You don't raise a Rottweiler by accident. You raise them with intent, with structure, and with the kind of grit most people never even knew they had. If you're still reading this—you're probably one of the rare few who gets it.

CHAPTER SEVEN:

HEALTH AND NUTRITION FROM PUPPY TO SENIOR

Feeding a Rottweiler is a long-term strategy, not a set-and-forget task. At each stage of life—puppy, adult, and senior—the dog's nutritional needs change in measurable ways. These shifts aren't superficial. They determine whether the dog develops properly, holds condition, avoids disease, recovers from injury, maintains cognitive function, and lives out its full potential lifespan. Most owners don't feed with that level of intentionality. They feed based on convenience, marketing, or habit. That's how preventable problems begin. This chapter is not about trends or theories. It's about what works, what breaks, and what you need to do differently if you want to raise a dog that holds up under pressure.

Puppy nutrition is where most owners go wrong, and the consequences usually don't surface until later. Rottweilers are a large, fast-growing breed. That means every nutrient given to a puppy affects joint development, cartilage stability, and long bone growth. An error in mineral balance or caloric density doesn't just result in temporary digestive upset. It has orthopedic consequences. This is not an exaggeration. Poor nutrition in the first year can lead to hip dysplasia, elbow dysplasia, angular limb deformities, and lifelong pain. It also leads to expensive surgeries, reduced mobility, early arthritis, and shortened working life. The solution is simple but non-negotiable: feed a properly formulated large breed puppy food and control both portions and growth rate aggressively.

This food must be labeled as large breed puppy. Not "all life stages." Not generic puppy chow. Not whatever's on sale at the big box store. You're looking for controlled calcium levels (1.0% to 1.5%), a calcium-to-phosphorus ratio between 1:1 and 1.3:1, and moderate fat and calorie density. If the food doesn't have feeding trials or published nutrient profiles, it's off the list. Stick with brands that hire board-certified veterinary nutritionists and back their formulas with real science. Purina Pro Plan, Royal Canin, Eukanuba, and Hill's Science Diet meet this standard. Most boutique brands do not.

Feeding schedule matters. Rottweiler puppies should eat three times per day until six months old. After that, two meals per day is appropriate unless your veterinarian advises otherwise. Free feeding—leaving food out all day— is a mistake. It leads to overeating, irregular digestion, and often weight gain. Use a measuring cup or scale. Portion control is not optional. Rottweilers are opportunistic eaters. They will over-consume if allowed, and you won't know it's a problem until the damage is already done.

During this phase, you're feeding for slow, steady growth. Not bulk. Not size. Not appearance. Rottweiler puppies that look "thick" at 12 weeks are almost always overweight. A lean, athletic pup with visible waist definition and palpable—but not visible—ribs is ideal. If you need to press to find ribs, the dog is too heavy. If the dog has fat rolls around the neck or shoulders, it's well past the ideal range. Do not assume the puppy will "grow into it." That line has ruined more dogs than poor breeding ever has.

Stick to the same food for at least three to four months unless your vet recommends otherwise. Dogs don't need variety. Switching foods frequently increases the risk of digestive upset and makes it harder to track the impact of the diet. If the dog develops diarrhea, soft stools, or excessive gas, consider whether food changes, treats, or supplements may be the cause. Puppies don't need extras. No table scraps, no raw bones, no untested supplements. More is not better. Balanced is better.

Water intake must be monitored as well. Puppies eating dry food require constant access to fresh, clean water. Add water or broth to meals if you're concerned about hydration. Dehydration in puppies contributes to fatigue, concentration of toxins in the kidneys, and reduced joint lubrication. Clean food and water bowls daily. Bacteria builds fast, and puppies have weaker immune systems than adults.

By 12 to 18 months, depending on growth rate and individual condition, your dog will transition from the puppy stage into early adulthood. This is where the next mistake often happens. Owners assume the dog is "grown," switch to adult food, and increase meal size. That often results in a spike in weight, a drop in physical output, and a gradual decline in joint health that gets misinterpreted as personality changes or laziness.

Transition to adult food should be based on vet recommendation or a clear slowing of physical growth—not just age. Do it gradually over 10 to 14 days. Start with 25% new food, 75% old, and shift in stages while monitoring stool quality and energy levels. If the transition causes vomiting or diarrhea, slow it down or consult your vet. During this time, recheck your feeding portions. Adult foods often have different calorie density than puppy formulas. Feeding the same volume is a common mistake.

From 18 months to roughly 6–7 years is the adult maintenance phase. Here, the dog should be at peak condition—lean, muscular, energetic, and mentally sharp. The goal is to maintain that condition through correct portioning, appropriate protein and fat intake, and adjustments based on season, activity level, and weight trends. This stage requires vigilance. Rottweilers can gain weight quickly and shed it slowly. You'll notice when the collar feels tight or the dog pants after a short walk, but by then it's already an issue. Prevention is easier than correction.

Weigh your dog monthly if possible. If not, track photos from a consistent angle. Look for early signs: loss of waist definition, jiggling skin when walking, a general "blocky" appearance that isn't muscle. If in doubt, cut portions by 10% for two weeks and reassess. No dog gains weight on air. If your dog is getting heavier, you're feeding too much or exercising too little—or both.

Daily exercise is not a substitute for proper feeding. Many owners try to "work off" excess calories instead of adjusting intake. That's backwards. A well-fed dog that gets moderate exercise will stay in better shape than a dog that eats too much and runs to compensate. Exercise should support feeding, not fix it.

Use the tools. Slow feeders for dogs that inhale meals. Puzzle bowls and snuffle mats for dogs that need mental stimulation. Food-dispensing toys for dogs with destructive tendencies. Every bite of food is an opportunity to build habits, reinforce structure, and maintain calmness. Don't waste it by dumping kibble in a bowl and walking away.

This stage is also where owners get lazy. They start adding treats, table scraps, high-calorie chew items, and unbalanced "extras" to the diet. All of that counts toward the dog's total daily intake. A few slices of cheese here, a scoop of peanut butter there, and suddenly your 95-pound Rottweiler is carrying 10 pounds of useless fat on their joints. Treats should be part of training, not a substitute for attention or a bribe for behavior. Use the dog's own kibble as a reward when possible. If using commercial treats, choose low-calorie, single-ingredient options. Measure everything.

Feeding isn't just about the dog's preference. It's about long-term performance. A lean dog will live longer, move better, and recover faster from injury or illness. A heavy dog is a liability. The excess weight increases risk of cruciate ligament tears, back injuries, hip pain, and heart stress. It also increases the cost of care. An overweight dog needs more sedation for surgery, more medication per dose, and more monitoring for complications. Fat is not harmless. It is a chronic health threat.

Around seven years of age, your Rottweiler enters the senior phase. This doesn't mean the dog is old and fragile, but it does mean that metabolic changes are happening behind the scenes. Recovery slows. Muscle mass begins to decline. Cognitive changes may begin. At this stage, every calorie matters. The feeding goal becomes preservation of function, not just weight control.

Switching to a senior food is not always required, but the diet must now support joint health, brain function, kidney support, and immune resilience. Look for higher-quality protein sources, lower phosphorus, and added omega-3s. Most "senior formulas" on the shelf are low-protein, high-carb filler products. Avoid them. You may be better off adding targeted supplements to your current adult food than switching formulas. Talk to your vet and base the decision on bloodwork and physical condition, not a number on the calendar.

Monitor muscle mass, especially in the hind end. If your dog begins losing tone in the rear legs, don't assume it's just age. That's a marker of disuse, joint pain, or nutritional deficiency. Adjust exercise to include low-impact movement like structured leash walks, uphill walks, or hydrotherapy if available. Maintain weight-bearing activity as long as the dog is mobile. Muscle that's lost is hard to regain. Don't wait until it's gone.

Appetite often drops in senior dogs. If your dog stops eating or becomes picky, investigate. Dental pain, organ dysfunction, and cognitive decline can all present as food refusal. Softening food or adding broth is fine, but don't cover symptoms with convenience. Rule out medical causes first. A senior dog should still be interested in food unless something is wrong.

Hydration becomes critical in senior dogs. They dehydrate faster and often drink less. Add moisture to meals, keep water bowls in multiple locations, and monitor urine output. Reduced water intake contributes to constipation, urinary tract issues, and kidney strain. If you're feeding dry kibble only, assume your dog is borderline dehydrated unless proven otherwise.

At all stages, ignore food trends that are not supported by science. Raw food, boutique blends, grain-free hype, exotic protein marketing—none of these belong in your feeding plan unless a board-certified veterinary nutritionist tells you otherwise. Most raw diets are unbalanced. Most boutique brands don't do feeding trials. Grain-free diets have been linked to heart disease in large breed dogs. If your dog has a diagnosed allergy or condition, that's different. But if you're feeding based on labels or online anecdotes, you're gambling.

Your job is to feed for structure, health, and long-term performance. That means science-based nutrition, portion control, hydration, condition tracking, and consistency. Nothing fancy. Nothing emotional. Just what works.

You're not raising a food critic. You're building a working animal with high physical and mental demands. The food you choose today is either building their future—or breaking it down in silence.

CHAPTER EIGHT:
VETERINARY INSIGHTS

Here's the part that separates the owners who actually give a shit from the ones just winging it on vibes and grain-free marketing slogans: health.

You didn't buy a lapdog. You didn't adopt a toaster with fur. You took on a brick-built working breed with more horsepower than common sense, and enough genetic landmines to turn complacency into catastrophe. So let's get one thing straight from the jump—owning a Rottweiler isn't just about exercise, food, and flexing your dog's "drive." It's about looking ten miles down the road and making sure they actually live long enough to enjoy the damn journey.

Start with the body. The Rottweiler frame is a walking paradox: compact, muscular, dense—but fragile in all the wrong places. You want to know where this breed fails first? Hips and elbows. Every. Fucking. Time.

Even with a rock-solid pedigree, perfect food, and all the right supplements, it's not uncommon to see joint wear before age six. And if you got your dog from a backyard breeder who thought "health testing" meant checking if the parents were alive? Good luck. Hip dysplasia is practically a family heirloom in this breed. Elbow dysplasia isn't far behind. They both work the same way: shitty joint construction, instability, pain, and progressive arthritis that doesn't go away, just gets meaner with age.

And let's talk about the one that hits fast and hits hard: cruciate ligament rupture. Cranial cruciate, if you want to sound fancy. It's the dog version of an ACL tear. And unlike dysplasia, this one doesn't give you a warning. One bad landing. One hard turn. One slip on tile. Boom—dog screams, won't bear weight, and suddenly your quiet afternoon is now a $5,000 surgery consult.

Oh, and if you ignore it or hope it "heals naturally," spoiler alert: it doesn't. You'll just blow the other knee trying to compensate. Ask me how I know.

So what prevents it? Two things. A lean dog and a strong ass. I'm serious. If your dog has a thick waistline and solid rear musculature, the odds of a torn cruciate drop dramatically. This is why I preach weight control like it's a religion. Not because I care if your Rottie has abs. Because fat dogs break faster. Fat dogs suffer earlier. Fat dogs die sooner.

Exercise isn't a hobby. It's fucking protective. You don't wait until the limp starts to take fitness seriously. You start day one and you never let up.

Now let's move up the chain. You know what's worse than a blown knee? A silent heart. And Rottweilers? Oh, they're gunning for that cardiology file before they turn six.

Cardiac disease is a killer in this breed—and it doesn't knock. It just walks in and wrecks your life. We're talking about two main culprits: aortic stenosis and dilated cardiomyopathy (DCM).

Aortic stenosis is usually congenital. Translation: your dog was born with it, and you won't know until they collapse in the yard chasing a ball. It's a narrowing of the heart's outflow tract, which forces the heart to work overtime to push blood out. Some dogs drop dead during exercise with zero symptoms. Others faint. Some cough. Some look fine until they're not.

DCM is worse in some ways. The heart muscle gets weak, floppy, and can't pump. Blood backs up. Fluid builds. Dog coughs. Breathes weird. Swells. Slows down. Eventually collapses. If you're feeding a boutique or grain-free diet and your Rottweiler suddenly has no stamina, no appetite, and seems "off," this might be why. Taurine deficiency has been linked to DCM. That's not Reddit nonsense—that's hard data. So if you're feeding trendy bullshit with lentils and blueberries but no actual heart support, congrats: your dog might be dying slowly because your kibble bag looked classy on Instagram.

You want to play it smart? Start with a basic echocardiogram between ages three and five. I don't care if they look fine. I don't care if the breeder said, "No heart problems in the lines." Most of the time, they don't know—

or they're lying. Catching cardiac disease early means medication might help. Catching it late means grief and guilt.

The bottom line? You don't wait for a cough. You check the engine before it stalls.

And now, the bastard you really need to prepare for: cancer. This one's not a maybe—it's a ticking fucking clock.

Rottweilers are one of the most cancer-prone breeds in North America. Lymphoma, osteosarcoma, mast cell tumors—you name it, they get it. You can feed the best food, keep them lean, exercise daily, and still watch them go down in six weeks from a tumor you didn't see coming.

Lymphoma shows up as swollen lymph nodes—jawline, neck, behind the knees. It can be fast. Like, fine on Monday, terminal on Friday fast. Chemo helps, but it's not a cure. You're buying time.

Osteosarcoma is a special kind of hell. Bone cancer. Usually starts with a limp that won't go away. You'll think it's a sprain. Then you'll get x-rays and the vet will go quiet. Amputation and chemo are standard, but survival's measured in months. Not years. Months.

Then there are mast cell tumors. These little bastards can look like anything—bug bites, pimples, cysts. Sometimes they stay put. Sometimes they spread like wildfire. Only way to know? Biopsy. You see a lump? Don't guess. Don't wait. Get it aspirated. Early removal saves lives. Delay kills dogs.

Here's the reality check: you don't wait for obvious symptoms in this breed. You don't get that luxury. You track everything. You notice when something's off. Appetite dip? Mark it. Limp? Time it. New lump? Aspirate it. Fatigue? Ask why. Rottweilers don't fake illness. They hide it until they can't. So if they slow down, if they change, if they look at you like something's wrong—it is. Trust them.

Now let's talk about the stuff that should be routine—but still gets fucked up because people get lazy. Vaccines. Parasite prevention. Dental care. You think these are minor? They're not.

Distemper, parvo, adenovirus, rabies—these aren't optional. They're the law, and they're the shield. You don't delay boosters because you're "natural." You don't skip vet visits because you read some herbalist's blog. If your dog interacts with other dogs, water, dirt, or literally anything outside your kitchen, they need coverage.

Lepto? If you have wildlife nearby or your dog drinks from puddles, it's a must. Bordetella? Boarding or daycare? Get it.

Titer testing? Sure, with a vet who knows what they're doing. Not because some YouTube channel said "big is lying."

Dental care is the one everyone ignores until the dog's mouth smells like a corpse and their molars look like fossils. You think it's just bad breath? No, genius—it's periodontal disease. That shit goes systemic. It'll rot their kidneys, trash their heart, and put them in pain long before they whimper. Brush. Use chews. Get cleanings. If your dog drops kibble, drools weird, or avoids chewing, get the vet to look.

And don't get me started on fleas, ticks, and heartworm. One fucking mosquito bite is all it takes. You want to skip prevention because "they're mostly inside"? Cool—hope you've got five grand saved for heartworm treatment. One tick bite can tank your dog's joints. Use prevention. Monthly. No excuses. You're not being holistic. You're being cheap.

Now let's go there—the spay/neuter war. Everyone's got an opinion. Most of them are garbage.

For decades, the default was to cut 'em at six months. But newer research—real, peer-reviewed data—says that's probably a mistake for large breeds like Rottweilers. Early sterilization messes with hormone development. That means more joint issues, higher risk of osteosarcoma, incontinence, weaker musculature. For real.

So what's the move? Wait. 18–24 months minimum, ideally after full physical maturity. That means, yes, managing heat cycles in females and testosterone in males. It's inconvenient. It's messy. But it might save their joints and reduce their cancer risk down the road.

For females, that means bleeding, mood swings, and vigilance. Don't be a dumbass—if she's in heat, keep her contained. You're not a backyard breeder, right? Then act like it.

For males, it means managing drive. Testicle-driven stubbornness. Marking. Extra edge in behavior. If you can't handle that? Fine. Neuter—but later. Don't use surgery as a shortcut for structure.

And if you're keeping them intact long-term? Cool. Better have bombproof recall, leash control, and no behavioral bullshit. If your intact male is marking your couch or lunging at other dogs, congratulations, you've forfeited your right to avoid the snip.

It's not about morality. It's about management. Use the tool—don't worship it.

And finally, here's the hardest skill to build: knowing when to act and when to wait. Most emergencies don't show up with sirens. They whisper. A limp. A refusal to eat. A weird look. A stumble. Rottweilers don't whine. They don't cry. They endure. And by the time you notice they're off? You might be halfway to crisis.

The rule is simple: if something seems off and doesn't fix itself in 24 hours—call your fucking vet.

You're not overreacting. You're doing your job.

And if it's more serious—labored breathing, pale gums, sudden collapse, bloated abdomen? Get in the car. No waiting. No Googling. Just move.

Your Rottweiler is a tank. But tanks break too. And when they do, you don't get second chances.

Your job isn't to be paranoid. It's to be prepared.

CHAPTER NINE:
DAILY CARE AND ROUTINE

Here's the first lie that fucks people up: "Daily care just means food and a walk."

No. That's basic survival. That's the floor. That's how you raise a houseplant with a pulse. Caring for a Rottweiler—*really* caring for one—isn't about keeping them alive. It's about giving them a life they can actually survive in. And to do that, you don't need 900 gadgets or boutique dog food blessed by Himalayan monks. You need structure. You need rhythm. You need to stop letting chaos call the shots.

This chapter is the no-glamour manual. It's the part nobody brags about on Instagram. Because daily care isn't cute. It's relentless. It's brushing when you're tired. It's clipping nails on a Sunday night. It's being a little boring—every single fucking day—so your Rottweiler isn't.

Let's start with the obvious: the coat.

At first glance, you think, "Nice. Short hair. Low maintenance." Bullshit. Rottweilers have a double coat. Thick-ass undercoat beneath short, spiky guard hairs that cling to everything you own. It's not just shedding—it's shedding with vengeance. Twice a year, it blows out like a goddamn snowstorm made of regret. The rest of the time? It's still falling, just sneakier.

Brushing is non-negotiable. Not for vanity—*for health*. You're stimulating the skin, circulating oils, loosening dirt, and checking for problems. You know when I found Titan's first hot spot? While brushing. You know when I found a weird lump on his ribs? Brushing. You don't find these things while you're binge-watching Netflix with your dog curled next to you, covered in dead hair and secrets.

Tools? Rubber curry brush. Undercoat rake. Something that gets down into that dense mess and actually does work. Two or three times a week, minimum. More during coat blow season unless you like eating fur for breakfast.

Bathing? Chill the fuck out. This isn't a poodle. If you're bathing your Rottweiler every week, you're asking for skin problems. Once every six to eight weeks—unless they rolled in goose shit or decided to body slam a dead opossum. Use unscented shampoo, rinse like your life depends on it, and *dry thoroughly*. That dense coat traps moisture like a swamp. Let it fester and you'll be dealing with hot spots that smell like moldy gym socks. Invest in a dog-safe blow dryer if you're not about that mildew life.

Now nails. You already know. If you hear clicking on hardwood, you're already late. Long nails = shifted posture = stressed joints = arthritis = avoidable pain. Clip 'em every week or two. Use a grinder if you're scared of quicks. I don't care if your dog hates it—do it more often and they'll stop. Frequency breeds normalcy. Skip it for a month and the next trim feels like a mugging.

Feet matter. Feet are what carry your dog through everything else you want them to do—obedience, protection, hiking, whatever. And if those nails are curling like talons because you "forgot," then congrats: you're the reason your dog limps at age five.

Let's move up to the ears. Yeah, they're floppy. Yeah, they look cute. You know what else they are? Moisture traps. Heat traps. Bacteria breeding zones. Clean them *weekly*. Get a vet-approved rinse. Fill the canal, massage the base, let your dog shake like a maniac, then wipe the outer ear. Don't go digging inside with Q-tips like an idiot. Don't use alcohol like a psychopath. Just clean the damn ear. If it smells like bread, it's probably yeast. If it smells like roadkill, get to the vet. Now.

You know what's more common than you think? Chronic ear infections that go untreated until the dog ruptures an eardrum and starts tilting its head like it's high. All because someone couldn't be bothered to check once a week.

Now teeth. The part nobody wants to deal with because "it's hard" or "they hate it." Guess what? So do I. You think Titan loved getting his teeth brushed the first 20 times? Nope. But now he stands there like a champ because we built the routine. You brush a few times a week, with enzymatic toothpaste—**not** your minty human shit unless you want to give your dog the runs.

Brushing isn't about making teeth sparkle. It's about controlling bacteria before it destroys the gums and migrates to the kidneys, the liver, or the heart. Dental care isn't cosmetic—it's systemic. And if your Rottie does any kind of gripping, carrying, or bite work? You better make damn sure those teeth don't hurt every time they close their jaw.

Dental chews? Cool—if they're not rocks. Too hard, and you'll fracture teeth. Raw bones? Maybe. Depends on your dog. Supervise like a hawk. The goal is clean, not broken.

Alright. Let's talk about the elephant in the room: **exercise**.

I'm gonna say it flat out—if your Rottweiler isn't getting daily, structured physical and mental stimulation, you are fucking up. Full stop.

This isn't a breed you can park in a backyard and call it enrichment. That's like locking a pro athlete in a room with a yoga mat and thinking they'll thrive. Zoomies and random sprints aren't the same as real movement. Unstructured play is not a substitute for command-based exertion.

One hour minimum, every single day. Ideally split into two or three sessions. Morning leash walk with expectations. Midday flirt pole, drag work, or obstacle challenges. Evening mental games—scent work, tug with rules, place drills. Doesn't need to be fancy. It needs to be **consistent**.

Why? Because movement regulates stress. It drains tension. It clears the mental fog that turns into fence-fighting, reactivity, destruction, and twitchy guarding. A calm Rottweiler isn't necessarily *relaxed*. They might just be mentally locked up with nowhere to go—and you'll find out the hard way when they explode over a squirrel or a knock at the door.

And if the weather sucks? Adjust. Don't cancel. Hot? Go early. Go late. Keep it short but focused. Carry water. If your dog's panting like a freight train, glazed eyes, stumbling—you're too late. Get them cooled down. Cold? Put on a vest. Salted sidewalks? Booties. Snowed in? Welcome to treadmill season. Teach it young. Make it part of the rhythm. Don't wait until you're desperate.

Mental stimulation is what really separates the "tired" from the *satisfied*. A Rottie that's physically exhausted but mentally bored is still a liability. They'll chew through a crate, launch over a fence, or dismantle your living room with the intensity of a demolition crew. You gotta work that brain.

Structured obedience drills. Impulse control work. Scent games. Puzzle feeders. Down-stays under pressure. Send to "place" with the doorbell ringing. Move obedience into new locations. Repetition *with relevance*. You're not raising a dog. You're managing a tiny military unit that just happens to nap on your floor.

And no, they don't need constant novelty. They need routine. That's the difference. Routine doesn't mean robotic. It means stable. It means reliable. It means *safe*.

Speaking of routine—this is where most people fail. They start strong, then get "too busy." Things slip. Morning walk becomes afternoon sprint. Meals shift. Rules bend. Crate time disappears. And guess what? Your dog notices. Every slip. Every delay. Every "fuck it, just this once." You think it's minor. Your dog thinks the structure is broken.

You want to know what's more powerful than any single correction, drill, or command? **Predictability.** Dogs don't need variety. They need to know what happens next.

Feeding at the same times every day. Walks with rhythm. Rest that's enforced. Training that's expected. Crate time as part of the plan—not punishment, not neglect, but decompression. You're not programming a robot. You're setting the tempo for a nervous system. Rottweilers with stable routines don't flinch at loud noises, don't overreact to changes, and don't make your life hell because they "suddenly" forgot how to act.

You know what else routine gives you? **Early detection.**

If your dog eats every meal, every day, and suddenly skips one? That means something. If they move with rhythm, and now they're limping on the stairs? That's a flag. If they always go nuts for tug and now they don't care? That's not a mood swing—it's data. Routine gives you a baseline. And when you know your baseline, you know when the machine is starting to fail.

Now let's get uncomfortably honest. If your Rottweiler is showing "problem behaviors," but you're skipping care days, delaying walks, ignoring signs of stress, brushing once a month when the mood strikes, and calling it good because "he seems fine"—you're not doing your job.

Not because you don't love your dog. Because you're half-assing the commitment. And this breed? It doesn't play nice with half-assed.

Daily care *is* the relationship. Not the play. Not the show-off moments. The grind. The repetition. The boring shit you do when nobody's watching. That's where the bond builds. That's where your dog learns trust, rhythm, regulation, and control.

Skip it, and here's what you get:

- Chewed baseboards.
- Dug-up gardens.
- Fence fights at 6 a.m.
- Torn-up beds.
- Shredded couches.
- Window barking.
- Guarding shadows.
- Mounting guests.
- Eating batteries.
- Pacing all night.
- Destroyed toys in 30 seconds.
- Eating socks.
- Crate breakouts.
- Screaming at doorbells.
- Stealing food.
- Waking you up to puke garbage.
- Scratching until they bleed.
- Starting fights with nothing.

None of that comes from a "bad dog." It comes from unmet needs.

You don't fix this shit with dominance. You don't fix it with a stern voice and a longer leash. You fix it by doing the fucking work. Every day. Like clockwork. Because every time you skip? Your dog *notices*. And every time you show up, even when it sucks? They feel that too.

Rottweilers don't need perfection. But they demand consistency.

So build the rhythm. Brush. Bathe. Trim. Clean. Walk. Work. Play. Rest. Repeat.

You'll get tired. You'll feel like you're doing the same thing forever. That's the point.

The repetition doesn't wear your dog down—it *builds them up*. The boredom? That's your sign that things are finally stable. And when things are stable, your Rottweiler becomes the best version of themselves.

Not just a powerhouse. Not just a protector. But a balanced, grounded, predictable partner.

That's what daily care does. That's why this chapter matters.

This isn't optional.
This is the job.
So do it. Every damn day.

CHAPTER TEN:
BEHAVIORAL MANAGEMENT (WITH FAQs)

Rottweilers don't "just act out." They calculate, react, escalate—and they do it with purpose. That's what makes them incredible when handled right, and dangerous when they're not. You can't afford to treat behavioral issues like quirks. What looks like "just being stubborn" in a Lab can turn into a lawsuit in a Rottweiler. You're not managing mischief. You're managing drive, pressure response, and instinct layered over 100+ pounds of muscle that's genetically wired to protect, defend, and win conflict.

Let's get this out of the way early: every Rottweiler will test you. Every single one. Doesn't matter how well-bred they are. Doesn't matter if you raise them from eight weeks old, feed the best food, do puppy classes, and never miss a nail trim. At some point, they will challenge your authority. And if you flinch, hesitate, or default to emotion—you lose.

Not in a dramatic, Hollywood-style bite-your-hand-off way. In a quieter, more dangerous way. The moment your dog learns you can be negotiated with, avoided, or pushed around, the power balance starts to shift. And once that shift starts, it's hard—really hard—to reverse.

This doesn't mean you fight your dog. It means you lead them. Calmly, clearly, and without apology. If they challenge a boundary, you hold it. If they ignore a command, you don't repeat it ten times while hoping for a miracle. If they guard an item, a doorway, a person—you intervene early and decisively, not later when the damage is already done.

Guarding is baked into the breed. It's not a bug. It's a feature. But if you don't control the context, that feature becomes a liability. You'll see the early signs: freezing when someone approaches, stiff posture in doorways, hackles up when you hug someone, lip lifts around food or toys.

That's not protectiveness. That's insecurity wearing armor.

A well-bred, well-trained Rottweiler doesn't bark at everything. They observe. They assess. They hold pressure like a coiled spring—only engaging when truly needed. It's honestly kind of poetic when you see it in action.

You get that kind of control by socializing early, maintaining obedience under pressure, and exposing them to new people and environments with clear leadership. You don't teach your dog not to guard. You teach them what's theirs to guard—and what isn't.

That takes exposure, repetition, and clarity. Lots of it. If your dog barks at every guest or postman or jogger, they don't feel safe. And that's on you. Either you've failed to communicate that the situation is handled, or you've given them too much freedom to make decisions they aren't qualified to make.

FAQ: "How much barking is normal for a Rottweiler?"

Not much. This is not a vocal breed by nature. Alert barking? Totally fine. Persistent barking at everything that moves? That's not breed type—that's stress, lack of boundaries, or a dog taking over a job you never hired them for. If your Rottie is barking their head off at windows, people, noises, or even shadows, that's not "protectiveness"—that's unmanaged arousal.

The moment a Rottweiler starts making their own rules, the household stops feeling like a team. That's when you start seeing resource guarding—not just with food, but with objects, people, space. They growl when someone walks past their toy. They block you from the couch. They posture when you try to leash them.

These aren't isolated behaviors. They're a pattern forming. And if you ignore them, that pattern hardens.

The fix isn't screaming. It's structure. You want to prevent guarding? Control access. Work impulse control. Make the crate the default resting place. Teach trades with high-value rewards. Handle the food bowl daily. Take objects away, return them, and never let the dog feel entitled to possession.

This is not about dominating your dog. It's about removing ambiguity. Ambiguity is the root of most behavior problems in this breed. Your Rottweiler shouldn't wonder who owns the house, who sets the rules, or whether growling gets them what they want. That clarity creates safety—for them, and for everyone around them.

FAQ: "Is resource guarding ever just a phase?"

No. It's always data. It might look like a phase—come early, fade for a bit, then return later in adolescence with teeth and momentum. But any growling over possessions should be treated as a training opportunity, not a personality quirk. Catch it early, address it calmly, and don't cross your fingers hoping it'll vanish. Because it won't.

Separation anxiety hits this breed hard. They bond deeply, intensely, and fast. That's a gift when channeled correctly—but if you don't build independence early, you're setting yourself up for disaster.

A Rottweiler with no coping skills will scream, chew, scratch doors, pace endlessly, and try to break out of crates the second they're alone. That's not defiance. That's panic.

The fix? You start day one. Crate training isn't just for bedtime. It's a tool for teaching your dog how to settle without you. Short sessions. Door closed. You leave the room. You come back. You repeat. Don't make arrivals and departures emotional. No drawn-out goodbyes. No dramatic scenes. The dog needs to learn that your absence is routine, not a crisis.

If your dog already has separation issues, the solution isn't affection—it's desensitization. Gradual alone time. Layered exits. Predictable routines. And sometimes, medication in partnership with a behaviorist. Don't wait until your front door is chewed through or the crate bars are bent. Early intervention isn't a luxury—it's the only way forward.

FAQ: "Is it OK to let my Rottie follow me from room to room?"

It's normal—until it's not. Shadowing behavior can signal hyper-attachment. If your dog panics when the door closes behind you, or can't nap unless you're in sight, it's time to practice separation. You don't need to avoid them—but you do need to teach them how to exist without you for short stretches. That's not mean. That's mental health training.

Then there's dominance testing. The word "dominance" has been so abused that people either weaponize it or avoid it entirely. You don't need to be "alpha." You need to be stable. A Rottweiler will test boundaries the same way a smart teenager does—quietly, persistently, and always at the worst possible moment.

The tests are small. Ignoring a recall. Refusing to move off the couch. Blocking your path. Pushing into your space. They're not trying to overthrow the government. They're asking a question: Are you in charge, or am I?

Answering that question doesn't require yelling. It requires presence. Timing. Follow-through. If you ask for a behavior and don't get it—follow up. If the dog blocks your space, walk through them. If they challenge your leash pressure, hold the line. Every moment of hesitation is a vote of confidence for chaos. And chaos is exactly what this breed will create if you leave a leadership vacuum.

You also need to be aware of triggers. Is your dog more reactive on leash? In the car? At the front window? Around food? With certain people? Triggers aren't excuses. They're data. You manage them by limiting exposure while building coping skills. You don't flood the dog with chaos and hope for growth. You set up reps that teach recovery. That means controlled greetings. Pattern training. Mark-and-reward for looking at a trigger and disengaging. It means managing arousal—not suppressing it, not avoiding it, but guiding it into something productive.

Some dogs need more management than others. Some need pressure outlets daily. Some need structured avoidance of chaos until their confidence catches up. But all Rottweilers need leadership that doesn't flinch.

FAQ: "My dog barks and lunges on leash. Is that aggression?"

Not always. Leash reactivity often stems from frustration or fear—not intent to harm. But here's the catch: the world doesn't know the difference. If your dog is acting aggressive, you are responsible for the impression that creates. You fix this with behavior work, not with retractable leashes and wishful thinking.

And here's where most owners mess up: they wait too long to ask for help. They wait until the growling turns to snapping. Until the barking gets a complaint. Until the dog lunges at a jogger and the leash barely holds. They don't call a trainer when the red flags appear—they call when the consequences start stacking up.

There's a moment most Rottweiler owners don't see coming. It starts with a neighbor complaining about barking. Then it's a delivery person afraid to walk up the drive. Then it's a note from animal control. Then it's an injury—minor, but serious enough to turn into a record. And suddenly, it's not just your dog. It's a liability.

Here's when you call a trainer—before that happens:

Behavior   Why It Matters

Your dog growls when people walk near their toys, bed, or food   Early sign of resource guarding—needs structured intervention.

You can't take anything from their mouth without a fight Signals possession issues and lack of impulse control.

You can't touch their collar without tension   Indicates handling resistance and a trust or leadership gap.

They lunge or bark at people, dogs, bikes, strollers Possible leash reactivity or fear-based aggression.

You dread guests coming over   A sign your dog is controlling the environment or is overprotective.

You avoid certain walking times to dodge triggers You're managing, not training—time to reset.

You leave the TV on when you're gone because they scream without it   Classic separation anxiety—won't improve without guidance.

You feel like the leash is your only lifeline

You're relying on tools instead of trust and structure.

You feel anxious walking your own dog Your dog is leading, not following.

Your vet has "notes" about restraint or sedation

Even professionals are seeing red flags.

Your dog controls who can move around the house

Full-on space guarding—a serious behavior issue.

These aren't quirks. They're alarms. And waiting makes it worse. Don't wait for someone else to call the authorities. Call a qualified trainer—now.

This chapter isn't about making you paranoid. It's about handing you the tools before the spiral starts. Because once it begins, fixing it gets harder, slower, and more expensive. And every week you wait is a week the dog gets better at being unmanageable.

The good news? Behavior issues aren't a character flaw. They're a communication breakdown. Most of them can be managed—if not fully resolved—by shifting structure, fixing routines, increasing engagement, and reinforcing clarity. But you have to be honest about the dog in front of you. Not the one you wanted, not the one you see on Instagram, but the one that lives in your house.

You're not training a robot. You're building a relationship. One that says: I lead, you follow. I decide, you trust. I protect you, and you protect what I tell you to protect—nothing more.

A well-raised Rottweiler doesn't challenge everything. They challenge when leadership is absent. Fill the void, and the chaos disappears. Leave it empty, and the dog fills it with instincts you can't override with love alone.

You don't solve behavioral problems by loving harder. You solve them by showing up with a plan.

CHAPTER ELEVEN:
TRAINING TECHNIQUES FOR ROTTWEILERS

The first time a Rottweiler ignores you, it doesn't feel like a big deal. The second time, it's a little annoying. But the third time? That's the moment it should hit you like a brick to the skull: this dog isn't guessing. He's making decisions. And he's deciding you don't fucking matter.

That was Titan, my first Rottie—eight months old, built like a wrecking ball with a tongue. One afternoon, I called him back from the edge of the yard. He looked at me, tilted his head like he was weighing his options, then turned the other way and walked off. That wasn't confusion. That was a power play. And it worked, because I hadn't shown him that listening was non-negotiable. That moment—me, standing there with a leash in one hand and nothing in the other but shattered illusions—was the last time I treated training like a vibe.

You don't train a Rottweiler with optimism and a pocket full of treats. You train them with a plan. With structure. With the kind of relentless consistency that makes your friends think you're overdoing it. But you're not. You're surviving. Because this isn't a doodle who forgives your inconsistencies with tail wags and puppy eyes. This is a thinking, feeling, evaluating animal who's constantly reading your bullshit meter. If your words don't match your actions, if your cues don't come with clarity and follow-through, they'll decide they're better off running their own program. And once that contract breaks, good fucking luck getting it back.

Now let me be clear: positive reinforcement works. It absolutely works. But only if you actually understand it.

Most people treat it like sorcery. Show a treat, say a word, get a behavior. Cool. Until the dog isn't in the mood. Until the leash is off. Until someone drops a hotdog bun twenty feet away. Suddenly, the magic stops working and you're standing there like an idiot waving a piece of turkey while your Rottie ignores you like you're his ex.

Here's the fix. Treat food like currency. Make your dog earn every fucking bite. I hand-fed Titan for three straight weeks when I brought him home. Every kibble was earned. Sit. Look at me. Lie down. Name recognition. You do the job, you get paid. You ignore me, the bank closes. And that food didn't come out of my hand if I didn't see actual effort. No begging. No luring. Just transactional precision. You do X, you get Y. Not vibes. Not luck. Not hope.

That's how you build value. That's how you show your dog that being in sync with you is profitable. Not just because you have food, but because the pattern is unshakable. Consistency breeds clarity. Clarity breeds trust. Trust becomes reliability. And reliability, my friend, is the holy fucking grail of Rottweiler training.

Without structure, all you've got is bribery. And a bribed Rottie is just a power-hungry hustler who's figured out that the human is soft. You give a Rottweiler wiggle room, they will take the whole goddamn house—and the car keys, and your pride. Positive reinforcement works *with* boundaries, not instead of them.

But let's talk about where most people really eat shit: house manners.

You bring home a Rottie and think, "Let's let him settle in before we start training." Wrong. The dog starts learning the moment he walks through your front door. And what you teach him in that first week becomes gospel. If you let him jump on the couch uninvited, congratulations, he now owns it. If he can blow through doorways like a battering ram without you saying shit, guess what—he runs the perimeter now. If he hovers in the kitchen while you prep food, licking the floor and stalking your hands, and you think it's harmless? Welcome to entitlement. You've installed it yourself.

Titan tried it. Day three in the house, he jumped up onto the couch like he was checking for softness. One paw. Pause. Eye contact. The motherfucker was testing me. I calmly walked over, leashed him up, guided him off, and blocked re-entry. He tried again fifteen minutes later. Same result. Calm. Boring. Certain. By day five, he stopped trying. Not because I scared him—but because the rules were unbreakable. And in his mind, that made them real.

Same goes for thresholds. You don't let a Rottie launch through doors like a berserker. You teach them to pause, check in, wait for permission. Not for dominance. For discipline. For safety. For structure. I don't care if you live in a studio apartment or a ranch in Montana. Your door is the portal to temptation, risk, and chaos. If your dog thinks crossing that line is their decision, you're not in control. And without control, your rules don't mean shit.

Which brings us to the core commands—the lifelines. Recall, heel, stay, leave it. These aren't tricks. They're emergency brakes. Insurance policies. The reason your dog lives to see another day when everything goes sideways.

Recall, in particular, is either rock solid or completely useless. "He comes when he feels like it" is a death sentence in disguise. I started recall in the hallway. No distractions. Long line. One cue: "Come." If he came fast, he got a jackpot—food, praise, play. If he hesitated, the fun stopped. No repetitions. No nagging. No "come... come... come here... COME HERE TITAN PLEASE." Just one clean ask. And every single time I said it, I meant it. We built speed. Precision. Reps in new places. Parks. Trails. Near other dogs. Near trash. In wind, rain, and tourist traffic. Recall became instinct. Not because I was lucky. Because I put in the work.

Same story with "leave it." You start with food in your hand. If the dog snatches, you close it. If they pause, you open. You reward the hesitation, not the lunge. And then you build it into real life. Chicken wings on the sidewalk. Crumbs on the floor. A dead squirrel, mid-decomposition. If I say "leave it," Titan doesn't think. He disengages. Not because I screamed at him, but because I taught him that ignoring temptation equals freedom.

"Stay" took patience. It wasn't about freezing the body. It was about calming the mind. We started with ten seconds. Then thirty. Then minutes. Then noise. Movement. People. Food. Dogs. I dropped plates. Ran vacuums. Invited chaos. And if he moved? We reset. Calm. Silent. Unflinching. By the time he was a year old, he could hold position through anything short of an earthquake.

Heel was hell for the first six weeks. Titan thought walks were sled training. But I didn't jerk the leash or yell "heel" like a lunatic every five seconds. I made being near me the most rewarding place in the world. Pulling made everything stop. Heeling made everything fun. Simple math. Dogs get it. Eventually, the pulling stopped. Not because he feared correction—but because the equation was crystal clear.

And let's kill one more lie while we're at it. "He knows it, he's just being stubborn." No. He doesn't know it under pressure. If he can't do it when the baby's crying, the delivery guy's knocking, the neighbor's dog is barking, and someone just dropped a plate of spaghetti on the floor, then he doesn't fucking know it. Training doesn't count until it works under fire.

Every moment with a Rottie is a test. They're not being jerks. They're gathering data. If you cue something and let it slide, you've just trained them that sometimes, the rules don't apply. And if sometimes the rules don't apply, they'll always test to see if *now* is one of those times.

This is why training is full-time. You don't punch in for fifteen minutes a day and call it done. Every leash walk. Every guest at the door. Every meal. Every interaction is training. And if it isn't, you're leaving reps on the table— and your dog is filling in the blanks.

Now, once your foundation is locked in, once you've got control under pressure, manners at home, and obedience that holds in chaos, then you can think about advanced work. Not before. Rottweilers are working dogs. That doesn't mean they need a fancy job to feel fulfilled. It means their brain and body were built for purpose. If you don't give them that, they'll invent it. And their version of "a job" might be guarding the yard from butterflies, rearranging your furniture, or barking at joggers like it's an Olympic sport.

Advanced training can be incredible—protection sports, scent detection, service and therapy roles, competitive obedience, carting, tracking—but it only works when the dog has a foundation strong enough to support the pressure. You can't bolt sport training onto an untrained dog. It's like putting nitrous in a busted Corolla. They need the fundamentals, proofed, pressure-tested, and reliable.

And if you think you can skip all that? That you're the exception? That your Rottie is different? Let me tell you exactly how that ends: in lawsuits, in heartbreak, in dead dogs. Because every time someone says, "He's fine... until..." you already know how the story ends.

But here's the real problem. Most people never even get that far. They fuck themselves from the beginning because they believe complete and utter bullshit.

And since we're already here, gloves off, let's torch the five worst training myths that keep getting these dogs in trouble.

First one: "You have to show them who's boss." No, you don't. You have to show them who's consistent. Dominance posturing isn't training. It's insecurity with a side of ego. You don't need to alpha-roll your dog like you're reenacting a Nat Geo documentary from 1997. You need to lead calmly, consistently, and with clarity. If your dog only listens when you raise your voice or puff your chest, they're not trained—they're just avoiding conflict.

Next: "Don't train until six months. Let them be puppies." Right. Let them build six months of unfiltered, chaotic behavior, then try to un-teach it once they're strong, stubborn, and set in their ways. Genius plan. Training starts on day one. Not formal drills—but rules, structure, boundaries. You think you're bonding? You're not. You're letting a toddler build the schedule.

Then there's: "They'll grow out of bad behavior." Bullshit. They grow *into* it. That reactivity, that pushiness, that lack of impulse control—it doesn't disappear. It levels up. That cute jump at twelve weeks turns into a dangerous shoulder-check at twelve months. Stop pretending it's a phase. Start treating it like the start of a pattern.

Next lie: "Treats ruin training. They won't listen without them." No, dumbass. Treats teach behaviors. Then you fade them. That's called shaping and proofing. If your dog only works for food, you haven't finished training—you've just started. The issue isn't the food. It's your lack of follow-through.

And my personal favorite: "Let them win sometimes to build confidence." What the actual fuck does that even mean? Win what? Confidence comes from clear expectations, reps, and earned success. Letting your dog blow off commands so they "feel good about themselves" is how you end up with an entitled liability who only performs when it's convenient. You don't build confidence by letting them cheat. You build it by helping them work through the hard shit and come out on top.

Every one of those myths is a bomb under your training plan. And it doesn't go off right away. It ticks quietly while your Rottie learns to cut corners, bend rules, and push boundaries. Then one day—snap. The kid runs up. The gate's left open. The pizza hits the floor. And your "almost trained" dog reminds you that almost doesn't fucking count.

This breed doesn't accept maybes. They need certainty. And if you don't provide it, they'll go looking for it themselves. That's when accidents happen. That's when dogs get labeled "aggressive" for doing exactly what they were wired to do in the absence of guidance.

So do the fucking work.

Build the plan. Follow the reps. Enforce the rules. Reinforce the wins. Don't half-ass it. Don't make excuses. Don't wait for something to go wrong to realize your training was fragile. You don't get second chances with this breed. You get what you build—or what you let slide.

A well-trained Rottweiler isn't perfect. But they're predictable. Steady. Calm under pressure. Ready to handle the chaos of real life without becoming part of it. They're not soft. They're not easy. But when you've put in the work—when they're tuned into you like a frequency you don't even have to speak out loud—you get something rare. You get trust. Not just from them, but from everyone around you who sees the difference between your dog and the rest of the shit show.

CHAPTER TWELVE:
DOG SPORTS & ROTTIES

Nobody tells you this shit at the start. They hand you a leash, a bag of food, maybe a chew toy, and they smile like, "You'll do great!" They don't mention that owning a Rottweiler is like being gifted a Ferrari with a V12 engine and no brakes. It looks great parked. It's fun for five minutes. Then it starts revving at red lights, and before long, it's crashing through your living room window.

What they should say is this: *If you don't give that dog a job, he's going to build one out of your drywall, your patience, and your fucking sanity.* And nine times out of ten, the solution isn't more rules. It's more purpose.

That's where dog sports come in—not as some elite club for the overachievers, not as a trophy chase for people with too much money and not enough personality—but as your lifeline. Your one shot at giving that powertrain a track to run on before it rips apart everything you've built.

Here's the real truth no one wants to say out loud: most behavior problems in working dogs are just misplaced potential. It's not dominance. It's not trauma. It's not "he's just being stubborn." It's boredom. It's a smart, driven, genetically loaded dog stuck in a stupid, pointless, stimulus-deprived life. He was built for work. You gave him a couch. Now he's bouncing off the walls and chewing his own feet—and you're wondering if he needs more training. No. He needs a fucking mission.

And I'm not talking about a puzzle feeder or five minutes of fetch before dinner. I'm talking about sports. Real, structured, high-intensity, mentally challenging work that channels every ounce of instinct into something that won't get your ass sued or your house condemned.

Take Schutzhund. Or IPO. Or IGP—whatever you want to call it now. This is the working man's holy trinity: tracking, obedience, and protection. You want a calm, stable, bulletproof Rottie in public? Train for IPO. You want a dog that can bite on command but also heel past a baby stroller without blinking? IPO. You want your dog to learn how to deal with pressure—real pressure—and not melt like a snowflake in a toaster? You guessed it.

Now let me be clear before the idiots crawl out of their holes—this isn't about teaching your dog to "attack." If you think that's what Schutzhund is, kindly fuck off and go read a pamphlet. Protection sports aren't about turning your dog into a weapon. They're about control under chaos. About harnessing drive, stress, environmental stimulation, and turning it into something you can turn off with a word. It's obedience with consequences. Not just sit and down and stay. But *do it with a guy yelling in your face, cracking a whip, while your heart's racing and your mouth is full of adrenaline.*

You can't fake that kind of control. You build it. Repetition by repetition. Mistake by mistake. And let me tell you—your dog *loves* it. Because for once in his life, the work is worthy of his ability. It challenges him. It engages him. It drains the tank.

And if bitework isn't your jam—or your dog doesn't have the genetics for it—there's a hell of a lot more on the menu. Start with obedience trials. Sound boring? Good. You need boring. You need the kind of repetitive, brain-melting training that turns "down" into a reflex and "stay" into a religion. Rottweilers don't respect your wishes—they respect your consistency. Obedience trials are consistency made flesh. Heel means heel. Sit means sit. Not when they feel like it. Not when you have treats. Always.

And if your ego can take a hit, agility is next. Yes, I said it. Agility. No, your Rottweiler isn't a Border Collie. He won't fly over jumps like a feathered fairy. But he'll learn. He'll sweat. He'll work. And you'll watch this 100-pound muscle tank bend, pivot, sprint, and jump like a fucking ninja in armor. It's humbling. It's hilarious. It's exactly what he needs. Because agility isn't just about speed—it's about teamwork. It's about body control. It's about teaching your dog to listen to your movement, not just your mouth.

If agility feels too fast and IPO too intense, look into rally. It's obedience with motion. Signs, direction changes, pivot turns—it's like a GPS course for dogs. Keeps their brain turned on and their body in gear. Plus, it gives you structure. Something to train for. Something to show up to. And that right there? That's the missing piece for most owners. **The calendar. The commitment. The accountability.** You don't just "train when you have time." You train because there's a trial next month and you don't want to eat shit in front of a judge.

But let's not forget the old-school stuff—the work Rottweilers were built for. Carting. Draft work. Harness up, hook them to a sled, a wagon, a tire, a cinder block if you're in a pinch. Let them pull. Let them strain. Let them feel the burn in their legs and the weight in their chest. They're not meant to be showpieces. They're meant to move. To carry. To fucking matter.

You know what happens when a Rottie pulls weight? Their brain shuts up. The anxiety goes quiet. The reactivity fades. Because they're finally doing something that makes sense. Something that feels *right*. No barking at strangers. No pacing by the door. Just muscles, grit, and a job to do. You want calm in the house? Drag work in the yard.

Now if your dog has the right wiring—clean nerves, drive, control—get into real protection sports. PSA. Mondioring. French Ring. The technicality is brutal. The failure rate is high. But the reward? A dog that can work under pressure, off-leash, through chaos, and still be safe in public. You don't get that from treats and praise alone. You get that from reps, pressure, and proofing under stress.

And I know some people are already whining. "But I just want a pet. I don't have time for sports."

Cool. You also don't have time for a chewed-up baseboard, destroyed blinds, a lawsuit because your untrained dog body-slammed a kid, or a psychotic meltdown every time the mail truck comes by. You don't *have to* compete. You don't *have to* title. But if you own a breed with this much power and drive and *you're doing nothing structured*? That's neglect. Not legally. Not technically. But spiritually. You're starving the part of your dog that needs to work.

Here's the secret: you don't need a sport to win medals. You need it to survive.

Because if you don't give your Rottweiler a job, *they will invent one.*

And you are going to fucking hate what they choose.

They'll protect imaginary threats. Guard the hallway. Obsess over shadows. Patrol windows. Develop obsessions. Bark like maniacs at leaves, at air, at your grandmother. And if they're not the "active" type? Even worse. You'll get shutdown. Avoidant. Flat. They look calm but dead behind the eyes. Their spark goes. They just... exist. And you think they're fine, until one day they explode because a lifetime of unexpressed drive turned inward and rotted their mind.

There is no middle ground. There is no "good enough" when the brain and body are starving.

And that's exactly why sports work. Because they give the chaos a map.

They teach pressure management. They teach resilience. They teach recovery. They teach *you* how to read your dog before shit goes sideways. They teach your dog that the world has patterns. Expectations. Rules. Sports aren't the finish line. They're the framework.

And yeah, not all sports fit all dogs. Genetics matter. Structure matters. Temperament matters. But there's something for everyone. Rally for the soft ones. IPO for the bangers. Nosework for the thinkers. Agility for the movers. Carting for the tanks. Protection for the monsters with control. You don't need to be a badass. You just need to show the fuck up.

There's a reason the best-behaved Rottweilers you'll ever meet aren't the ones with the prettiest training videos. They're the ones who work.

Every week. Rain or shine. Win or lose. Trial or no trial.

They work.

Sidebar, not that you need one, but here it is where it belongs—right in your face:

You want to know what sports will save your sanity?

Here you go:

Tracking. You want to slow your psycho down? Teach him to scent track. Ten minutes of tracking burns more brain calories than an hour of fetch.

Weight pull. Builds confidence. Drains energy. And makes your dog feel like an absolute boss.

Rally. Fast feedback. Mental stimulation. Perfect for control freaks. Great for beginners who can follow a sign.

Carting. No equipment? Make your own. Nothing resets a reactive dog faster than dragging a loaded sled through a field.

Nosework. Indoors, outdoors, doesn't matter. Teaches focus. Builds independence. And gives anxious dogs a task that makes them feel competent.

That's your sanity pack right there. Pick one. Commit.

Because here's the end of the story: every single Rottweiler you'll ever meet is doing *something*.

They're either working for you, or they're working against you.

And if you leave that decision up to them?

You're not going to like the answer.

So stop pretending sports are optional. They're oxygen. They're therapy. They're the thing that keeps your dog grounded when the rest of the world is a screaming, overstimulating mess of noises, smells, and movement.

Dog sports aren't extra.

They're the fucking blueprint.

CHAPTER THIRTEEN:
TRAVELING WITH YOUR ROTTIE

Let's get something straight: traveling with a Rottweiler isn't just a logistical challenge. It's a fucking operation. This isn't shoving a Shih Tzu in a tote bag and catching a flight to Palm Springs. This is hauling around a muscular, intimidating, misunderstood tank of a dog through a world built for golden doodles and Yorkies in hoodies. And if you think that sounds like an exaggeration, you clearly haven't tried to check into a hotel with a Rottie while Karen at the front desk clutches her pearls and whispers "aggressive breed" under her breath.

But let's rewind and start where most Rottie owners first get slapped with reality: the car.

Car travel with a Rottweiler is a full-contact sport. First, there's the crate—or at least, there should be. Don't tell me your 110-pound dog rides shotgun. That's not cute. That's fucking negligent. You slam the brakes once, and your Rottie becomes a 110-pound cannonball through your windshield. They don't need to roam. They need to be secure. Crate in the back. Properly anchored. If a crash happens, you want that dog contained—not flying through the air, not flailing around injured and terrified while you try to get help. It's not just about obedience. It's about safety. Yours, theirs, and everyone else's.

And if you think your dog won't tolerate a crate, that's your failure, not theirs. Crate training starts at home. Travel is not the time to suddenly introduce it and hope for the best. That's how you end up pulled over on the side of the interstate while your Rottie screams like a banshee and chews through the seatbelt. No. You train it early. You reinforce it often. The crate isn't punishment—it's their space. Their den. Their fucking sanity box when the world outside the car gets too stimulating.

But even with the best crate setup in the world, you're not escaping the drool. Welcome to reality. Rottweilers, especially anxious or excited ones, can produce enough drool to coat your entire backseat in slime. Nervous about new environments? Cue the faucet. Crate trained or not, you're going to war against strings of spit that defy gravity and personal boundaries. If you don't have a stockpile of towels in your car, you're doing it wrong. You need drool rags, wipes, maybe even a spray bottle of diluted cleaner if your dog likes to fling snot onto windows like it's modern art.

And don't even get me started on car sickness. Some dogs just don't travel well—period. And no, cracking the window won't fix it. If your Rottie starts panting, drooling excessively, yawning, or whining as soon as the car moves, congratulations: you've got a car-sick dog. Talk to your vet. Get meds if you need them. Don't try to "tough it out" unless you enjoy cleaning up half-digested kibble off rubber mats while your dog watches in shame.

Plan your routes. Plan your breaks. This isn't a road trip with your college roommate—it's a fucking mission. You stop every few hours for potty breaks, water, decompression. Not at the edge of a gas station where the asphalt burns their paws and some jackass is revving his engine two feet away. You find shade. You find grass. You find calm. Your dog isn't a machine. Treating them like one is how you end up with stress diarrhea in your trunk and a dog who never wants to get in the car again.

And for the love of all things decent, don't roll up to someone's house or a public stop and just fling the crate door open. You do that, you better pray your dog doesn't bolt into traffic, fight another dog, or scare a child half to death. Car exits are structured. Period. You open the hatch. You leash up. You give a command. You release *when it's safe*. Not before. Not because your dog's "excited." Excitement doesn't make the rules—you do.

Now let's level up to the big leagues: air travel.

Here's the deal—if you don't absolutely have to fly with your Rottweiler, *don't*. I'm not saying it's impossible. I'm saying it's a bureaucratic, stressful, high-risk hellscape full of fine print, hidden fees, breed discrimination, and a very real chance that some underpaid airport worker will lose or mishandle the one living thing in your life that actually matters.

If your dog isn't under 20 pounds and able to fit under an airplane seat—which, spoiler, your Rottie is not—they're going in cargo. Not cabin. Not your lap. Cargo. With the luggage. With the noise. With the temperature fluctuations and the complete lack of human supervision. And you think your Rottie is confident enough to handle that? Maybe. But maybe not. And "maybe not" in this case means trauma. Panic. Injury. Even death. It's rare, but it happens, and when it does, you don't get a do-over.

If you're forced to fly—relocation, emergency, long-distance move—you need a plan that would make NASA jealous. First, call the airline. Then call them again. Then call them a third time and ask for a supervisor. Get everything in writing. Breed restrictions change. Cargo rules shift with weather. Some airlines won't take brachycephalic breeds. Others ban "dangerous" dogs entirely—which, according to them, includes your sweet, couch-loving Rottie because someone saw *John Wick* and freaked out.

You'll need an IATA-approved crate, which isn't cheap. It must be ventilated on all four sides. It needs hardware, not plastic snaps. It needs water bowls attached to the inside and labels on the outside. You need vet certificates, signed within 10 days of travel. You may need additional documentation depending on destination—especially if it's international.

That's assuming the airline doesn't just say "No Rottweilers allowed." Because many do. And you won't find out until you're two hours into booking and suddenly someone reads the fine print. You think I'm kidding? I had to cancel a $600 flight because Delta's system let me book but their cargo department flagged my dog's breed three days before departure. You know what they told me? "Try American Airlines. They like dogs more." Great. I'll add that to the list of random fucking variables I apparently need to memorize just to move across the country.

And say you actually make it on the flight. Your dog's in cargo. You're in seat 21B between a crying baby and a guy who smells like boiled ham. You don't get to check on your dog. You don't know if they made it on the plane until you land. You sit there for five hours wondering if the handler remembered to clip the crate door properly or if your Rottie is now roaming the tarmac like an airport cryptid.

When you land? Hope your airport has a designated animal claim area. Some don't. You'll wait while your dog sits in a warehouse. Maybe alone. Maybe scared. Maybe covered in their own piss because turbulence made them lose control. That's the gamble. That's the price of not driving. And no, ESA letters don't fix this. Rottweilers are not legally recognized service dogs unless they are actually trained and certified as such. Try to cheat that system and you might get fined, banned from flying, or have your dog seized.

And if you're still thinking, "Well I'll just bring them on vacation with me," here's another landmine: breed restrictions.

Hotels, Airbnbs, rental homes—they'll all take your money until you show up with a Rottweiler. Then suddenly the "pet-friendly" policy has an asterisk the size of Texas. And that's assuming you made it past the booking filters, which often don't even give you the courtesy of saying why your reservation was denied.

You know how many times I've called ahead, confirmed the dog policy, showed up, and still got hit with "Oh… *he's a Rottweiler*"? Too many. You can hear the tone change. You can see the shift in body language. Suddenly every scratch on the floor becomes your fault, and every noise from your room is a "disturbance." You'll spend more time justifying your dog's existence than you will relaxing. You'll walk him after dark to avoid judgment. You'll pay a pet deposit and still worry they're waiting to charge your card for "damage" he didn't cause.

And God help you if you're staying long-term. Rentals are another wall of discrimination. Even if your Rottie is perfect. Even if you have insurance. Even if you offer extra deposit. All it takes is one paranoid landlord or a neighbor who read half an article on "dangerous dogs," and you're fucked.

You'll hear all the excuses. "It's not me, it's the insurance." "It's just our policy." "We love dogs, just not *those* dogs." And you'll smile, grit your teeth, and look for somewhere else while someone with a biting, yappy, untrained Maltese gets welcomed with open arms because they fit the aesthetic.

Here's the sidebar, in case you're wondering what actually helps in all this: a solid travel kit.

You need a real crate—not a soft carrier, not a seatbelt harness. You need towels, water bowls, travel food containers, proof of vaccines, proof of training, vet contact info, and at least two forms of ID on your dog. One tag should say "Needs Space." One should say "Do Not Pet." You need backup leashes, a long line, high-value treats, and whatever meds your dog needs for motion sickness or stress. Bring scent items from home—a blanket, a toy— something that smells like you. It matters. You need structure for exits, for potty routines, for feeding. You need your dog to know how to hold a place, how to ignore strangers, how to load up without drama. You need a dog that's predictable under stress. Not perfect. *Predictable.*

Because that's what travel is—a stress test. A moving environment full of unpredictability. New smells. Loud noises. Sudden changes. Tight spaces. And if your dog has never experienced those things in training, they will fall apart when it counts. It's not about "being chill." It's about *being prepared.*

And if you're not prepared, stay home.

Because a Rottweiler that melts down in an airport doesn't just embarrass you—it hurts the breed. Every time one of us fucks it up, the rest of us pay for it. Another hotel adds a restriction. Another airline updates their policy. Another landlord says no. All because some dipshit thought their 100-pound dog didn't need manners in public.

So if you're gonna travel with your Rottie, do it right. Train early. Plan obsessively. Advocate relentlessly. And carry yourself like someone who understands that the world doesn't make space for this breed—you have to carve it out.

Every gas station, every rest stop, every lobby, every TSA line is a test.

Pass it. Or stay the fuck home.

CHAPTER FOURTEEN: ROTTWEILERS AND FAMILY LIFE

Let's kill the fantasy right up front: **your Rottweiler is not a fucking nanny.** That Victorian fever dream of a slobbery, droopy-eyed canine Mary Poppins raising your kids while you scroll Instagram? Yeah. Dead. If that's what you want, buy a stuffed animal and pray to the ghost of Peter Pan. Real life doesn't work like that. Rottweilers are not babysitters. They are not magical guardians born to love your children more than their own survival instincts. They're working dogs with serious drive, serious strength, and zero tolerance for unpredictable bullshit unless you train, manage, and supervise like your sanity depends on it—because it fucking does.

Here's the first rule of Rottweilers and kids: **they don't mix safely by default.** This isn't a Labrador. This isn't some floppy rescue mutt bred for generations to tolerate toddlers riding them like ponies. This is a breed built for drive, defense, and task completion—not chaos, shrieking, or sticky fingers digging into ears. I'm not saying Rotties can't live with kids. I'm saying *you* have to be worth a damn at parenting both species if you expect it to work.

Kids don't come with built-in dog safety programming. They pull tails. They fall on dogs. They grab collars. They scream in ears. They run in circles like prey animals. Your Rottweiler sees that and doesn't think, "Aww, what a cutie!" He thinks, *That thing is unstable and I should correct it.*

And guess what? Rottweilers *correct* with teeth.

So let's be real. You want your Rottie and your kid to live under the same roof without someone ending up on the news? Supervise like a psycho. Manage like a tyrant. Set boundaries so tight they squeak. You don't just "hope for the best." You structure the best. No kid should be climbing on the dog. No kid should be grabbing ears or hugging. No dog should be left alone with a baby. I don't care how well-trained they are. I don't care if "he would never." They're dogs, not philosophers. They react. One startled growl becomes a bite, and one bite becomes your lawsuit—or worse.

Your kid doesn't get a free pass just because they're small and cute. If your child can't respect a dog's space, the problem isn't the dog—it's you. Teach the damn kid. "Don't touch while sleeping." "No food sharing." "No grabbing toys out of the dog's mouth." You think that sounds harsh? Let me tell you what's harsher: your kid getting a facial reconstruction because you didn't feel like supervising snack time.

And while we're at it—yes, Rottweilers can be absolutely wonderful with children *if* raised with clear structure, early exposure, and consistent correction for overexcitement or possessiveness. But that takes work. Daily work. Not vibes. Not luck. If your idea of management is yelling "No!" from the couch while your toddler tries to ride the dog like a sled, pack it in. You're the liability, not the Rottweiler.

Now let's talk about multi-dog households. Because for some reason, people get one Rottie, survive the first year, and think, "Let's get another!" as if they've mastered the dark arts of canine diplomacy. Spoiler: you haven't. One Rottweiler is a challenge. Two is a balancing act with a live grenade. More than that? You better have experience, structure, and a pair of steel balls because *shit gets real fast.*

Rottweilers don't form "packs" like some wolf documentary would have you believe. They form relationships. Individual, nuanced, often tense relationships based on hierarchy, confidence, and your leadership. They're not automatically "social." Many are dog-tolerant at best. Some are downright dog-intolerant after puberty hits. That sweet eight-month-old puppy who loved every playdate? At two years old, he might suddenly decide no other male is allowed to breathe his air—and if you're not ready to manage that, you're in for blood and vet bills.

Introducing a second dog into the house isn't about throwing them in the yard and "letting them figure it out." That's how you end up with trauma, injury, and long-term behavioral damage. It's slow. It's structured. Leashed walks together. Parallel play. Controlled environments. No toys. No food. No pressure. You don't test the dynamic by waiting for a fight—you test it by watching body language, thresholds, fixation, and tolerance.

And you don't let them "work it out" if tension builds. You step in. You interrupt. You reset. You advocate. Because once dogs decide the relationship is adversarial, you don't just hit rewind. You manage forever. That means crates, rotations, barriers, gates, and the willingness to separate for life if necessary. You ready for that? Or are you still dreaming of Instagram reels with matching bandanas?

And yes, same-sex aggression is a thing. It's real. Especially with males. Two intact males? You better be a fucking wizard. Even neutered, the tension can stay. Doesn't matter if they're brothers. Doesn't matter if they were raised together. Puberty hits, hormones shift, and boom—your living room becomes a war zone. Can it work? Sure. With the right dogs and the right owner. But if you're not both, don't try to play God.

Now let's get to the part everyone sugarcoats: **cats and small pets.**

Here's the unfiltered truth—**prey drive is real, and your Rottie isn't above it.** You may think they're gentle giants. And they can be. But they're also working dogs with genetic wiring that says, *"Small, fast, and squeaky = chase and kill."*

Yes, some Rottweilers live peacefully with cats. Others stalk them like a chew toy on legs. You won't know which you've got until one of them makes a move. That's not a gamble you get to take lightly.

Introductions are slow, leashed, and closely monitored. You watch the eyes. The posture. The breathing. Your Rottweiler fixates on the cat, freezes, ears forward, tail high? That's not curiosity—that's a red flag. You don't leave them alone together. Ever. You don't assume they'll "learn to get along." You create zones. You separate when unsupervised. You train impulse control like your cat's life depends on it. Because it fucking does.

And don't even think about rabbits, hamsters, guinea pigs, ferrets. Unless you're a handler with experience controlling drive in high-prey breeds, that's a hard no. The margin for error is razor-thin, and one mistake can't be undone. You think that sounds dramatic? It's not. I've seen a Rottie snap a cat's neck in three seconds because the owner turned their back to answer a text. Not because the dog was "mean." Because instinct won. You want to play zookeeper? Get real about the risks.

Now onto the human element—**guests and visitors.** This is where most Rottie owners get cocky and pay the price. You get used to how your dog behaves with you. You get lulled into a false sense of control. Then your buddy drops by, walks through the door unannounced, and suddenly your well-trained dog is standing stiff, ears up, tail high, staring at them like a fucking threat. And guess what? To your Rottie, they are.

Because Rottweilers aren't Labrador welcome committees. They're territorial. They're selective. And they default to caution unless taught otherwise. That means guest management is not optional. It's required.

You don't just let people "walk in." You set the tone. You control the intro. Crate your dog. Put them in place. Leash them if needed. Let them see the guest, hear your tone, read the environment. You allow them to approach when calm, not when excited. You don't let guests pet your dog without permission. You don't let your dog jump, bark, or get pushy. And if your dog's uncomfortable? You send them away. Crate. Place. Reset.

This isn't about being friendly—it's about being safe. Because one lunge, one growl, one lip curl at the wrong time and *boom*, you're now the asshole with the "aggressive dog." Doesn't matter if the guest provoked it. Doesn't matter if it was a misunderstanding. Public perception isn't fair—it's brutal. And if your Rottie bites someone, even with cause, you don't get to explain your side while the stitches go in.

Guests need rules too. No reaching. No bending over the dog. No squeaky baby voices. No rough play. And if they can't follow that? They don't get to interact. It's not their house. It's your dog's territory, your responsibility, your outcome. Set the boundaries or deal with the fallout.

And let's loop back, just for a second, to kill this **"nanny dog" myth** one more time.

You know where that bullshit started? Old-timey stories and a handful of well-behaved dogs who tolerated kids because they had good handlers. Not because of magic. Not because of love. And definitely not because they were born with a soft spot for toddlers. It's propaganda wrapped in nostalgia. Dangerous as hell. Gets people bit. Gets dogs euthanized. Because when your kid pulls a Rottie's ear and gets snapped at, and you tell the vet "But I thought they were nanny dogs," what you're really saying is: *I believed fairy tales instead of doing my fucking homework.*

Here's the truth: your Rottweiler is only as safe, stable, and family-friendly as you've trained and managed them to be. They're not here to raise your kids. They're not here to babysit your guests. They're not here to tolerate chaos and nonsense because "they're part of the family." They are dogs. With teeth. With instincts. With limitations.

And if you don't honor those truths? You're the problem.

You want a Rottie to thrive in family life? Good. You can absolutely have that. But it means supervision, boundaries, management, training, and a zero-tolerance policy for laziness or wishful thinking.

Do that, and you'll have the most loyal, stable, reliable family dog you could ever ask for.

Fuck it up, and you'll have a tragedy.

Pick wisely.

CHAPTER FIFTEEN:
LIFE LOGISTICS WITH A GIANT DOG

Owning a Rottweiler doesn't end at training, feeding, and the daily ritual of scraping drool off your pant leg. That's the easy part. The part nobody warns you about? The invisible war you'll fight with the outside world just to be allowed to own your dog. Not because your Rottweiler's done anything wrong, but because they exist—and in the eyes of the public, that's enough.

Let's start with the most boring but most destructive enemy: **breed restrictions**. You don't get to exist with a dog like this without running into bureaucratic nonsense. Landlords, insurance companies, homeowner associations—none of them care how well-behaved your dog is, or how much work you've put into training. The second you say the word "Rottweiler," the tone shifts. Suddenly the lease isn't available. Suddenly they "forgot" to mention their pet policy excludes certain breeds. Or worse, they pretend there's no issue until the paperwork's signed, and then spring it on you later—usually once you're emotionally, financially, and legally invested in the situation.

Breed restrictions are a bullshit mix of corporate ass-covering and lazy fear. They exist not because your dog is dangerous, but because someone, somewhere, saw a headline and decided Rottweilers are bad for business. And insurance companies ran with it. Most won't insure properties that allow "high-risk" breeds—which means most landlords won't take the chance. Even if they want to. Even if they trust you. They're not going to jeopardize their coverage because your dog has a big head and cropped tail.

You'll spend hours on rental listings. You'll call places that say "pet-friendly" only to find out that doesn't include anything with jaws. You'll consider lying about the breed—

and if you do, let me be very clear: it might get you in the door, but it won't save you when shit goes sideways. If there's a complaint, a photo, an incident, or even a neighbor who just doesn't like the look of your dog, you're done. Eviction, fines, liability. Your dog gets labeled, and your life gets harder, fast.

Same thing happens with HOAs. You move into your nice suburban neighborhood. You've got a fenced yard. You've got a training plan. You think, finally, somewhere safe and stable to raise a dog like this. Then someone drops off a packet of bylaws written twenty years ago by a guy who got bit by a Chihuahua but blamed every working breed under the sun. And there it is, buried on page seventeen under "Rules and Enforcement"—no Rottweilers. No "aggressive" breeds. No exceptions.

The truth is, none of this is about your specific dog. It's about their silhouette. Their reputation. The way their body blocks light when they stand in a doorway. You walk a Rottie down the street and watch what happens—strollers cross. Joggers give you a six-foot buffer. Some nervous guy in a Patagonia vest makes a joke like, "Hope that leash is strong!" It's always the same. You learn to see the fear before it lands. You get used to it, but you never forget it's there.

And then you realize something darker: you're one incident away from being exactly what they expect.

That's the real weight of owning a Rottweiler in public. The leash isn't just for control—it's your lifeline to a lawsuit. One growl, one snap, one bad read of a situation, and it's not a "dog having a bad day." It's a violent animal. Dangerous breed. Aggressive. Unpredictable. You could have done everything right. You could have decades of clean history, titles, evaluations, therapy work, the whole fucking resume—and none of it matters the second someone screams and points.

And if your dog bites someone? Even in defense? Even because someone's off-leash dog charged? Doesn't matter. Not to the court. Not to the HOA. Not to the media. Your Rottie bites, and it's your fault. That's the world you live in now.

Let's break that down. Your dog bites a person. Or another dog. Doesn't kill. Doesn't maul. Just breaks skin. That's enough. Animal control gets involved. Maybe the police. Maybe a civil suit. At minimum, you're facing a quarantine period. Fines. Possibly your dog being labeled "dangerous." In some states, that label sticks for life, even after you move. In others, it's a death sentence. Mandatory euthanasia. No appeal.

Even if the bite was justified. Even if your dog was protecting you. Even if the other dog started it. The law doesn't work in your favor when you own a dog that's been pre-convicted by the public for existing. Welcome to the club.

So you learn to handle with eyes in the back of your head. You scan every block for loose dogs, uncontrolled kids, clueless owners with flexi-leashes and "he's friendly" on repeat. You walk wide arcs. You keep a tight heel. You condition your dog to a muzzle not because they need it, but because one day, someone's untrained mutt is going to get in your Rottie's face, and if there's a fight, you want to control what the world sees.

And speaking of muzzles, let's talk about what they *don't* mean. They don't mean your dog is aggressive. They don't mean you failed. They mean you understand the assignment. Because while some Golden Retriever owner is laughing at their dog's "funny little nip" at the vet, you're managing the optics of owning a breed that doesn't get to make mistakes.

None of this is fair. You know that. I know that. But fairness is irrelevant when your dog weighs more than some people's children and could, in theory, end a life if you let go of the leash at the wrong moment. That doesn't mean they *will*. But it means people assume they might. And when people get scared, they sue.

Which brings us to the next logistical noose around your neck: **insurance.**

If you own your home, your insurance policy might refuse to cover you the second they learn you've got a Rottweiler. If you're renting, your landlord's policy might block you. If your dog bites someone and you *don't* have coverage, or worse—you lied on your application and claimed "mixed breed" or "Lab"—they'll hang you out to dry when it's payout time. Doesn't matter how loyal they were taking your monthly premium. The second it costs them money, you'll be alone.

This is where you start learning the insurance company blacklists. Most major carriers have them, even if they pretend otherwise. Rottweilers. Pit Bulls. Dobermans. Akitas. Wolf hybrids. Anything with "guard dog" vibes gets red-flagged. Some will offer coverage but exclude any dog-related incidents. Others just flat out say no. You might get lucky with a local or independent provider that looks at history instead of breed, but don't expect that to be easy. And if you ever change providers, prepare to go through it all again.

It's not just about having a policy. It's about having a policy that *includes* your dog, explicitly. Call. Ask. Get it in writing. Don't trust the checkbox. Don't assume silence means permission. Because if something happens and your company claims you hid the breed? They won't just cancel you. They'll fight the claim and hang the liability on your neck.

The irony, of course, is that most of these precautions aren't necessary because of the dog. They're necessary because of people. Stupid people. Nosey neighbors. Lazy owners. Random joggers who think your dog shouldn't be allowed to exist in public because of a story they read once. And then, when their off-leash dog rushes yours, and your Rottie defends itself, you get blamed. Because they were the victim. Even though they weren't holding a leash. Even though your dog didn't escalate. Even though you had every legal and moral right to protect yourself and your animal.

So what's the answer? Lock your dog inside forever? Move to the woods? Live in fear?

No. The answer is owning the truth and preparing for it like a professional.

You train your dog to a higher standard than anyone else on your street.
You muzzle condition.
You keep records—of training, vaccinations, incidents.
You find the rare insurance company that doesn't treat your dog like a felony.
You talk to landlords *before* you move in.
You document everything.

You run what-if scenarios in your head so you're not surprised when someone's off-leash Goldendoodle ruins your walk.

Because when the hammer falls, you don't get a do-over. You get one chance to have done everything right.

And if you haven't?
You're not the one who pays the price.
Your dog is.

That's the weight. That's the cost of owning a breed like this. Not because they're bad. But because people assume they are.

If you can carry that weight—without bitching, without cutting corners, without pretending it's not real—
then you deserve this dog.

If you can't?

Pick another breed.

Because you're not ready for what this world throws at a Rottweiler owner. And your dog doesn't deserve to pay for your delusions.

CHAPTER SIXTEEN: ENRICHMENT BEYOND TRAINING

Training keeps the rules in place. Obedience keeps the leash walk civil. But if you think that's enough to fulfill a Rottweiler, you haven't lived with one yet. These dogs were not designed to be couch potatoes who know how to "sit" and "stay" and then spend twenty-three hours waiting to be useful again. You don't need a working dog if you're not going to let them work.

And no, "being a good boy" isn't a job. Neither is existing in your house like a furry coffee table.

You want peace? Give them purpose. Because nothing burns out a high-drive dog faster than boredom in a pretty house with no outlet. They might look calm—just lying around, snoring like a chainsaw—but that's not satisfaction. That's stagnation. And stagnation in a Rottweiler isn't just laziness. It's pressure building under the surface until it comes out sideways. Destruction. Rebellion. Shit behavior that shows up in bursts when their brain hits idle and their body doesn't have anything better to do.

So what do you do when training's done for the day and the leash walks aren't cutting it? You give your dog a *job*. A real one. With expectations, resistance, responsibility. The kind that taxes their brain and body and leaves them tired in a way fetch never will.

Backpacking is one of the easiest, most accessible jobs you can give a Rottweiler. And no, this doesn't mean wandering the Rockies in a tent with a compass. It means putting weight on their back and walking with purpose. You get a good harness, fit a pack, and add a few pounds—nothing crazy at first. Let them carry bottled water. Poop bags.

Maybe their own kibble. The goal isn't cardio. The goal is mental engagement. The minute you put weight on them, they shift into a different gear. They stop sniffing every leaf. They walk straighter. They stay more tuned in. Because they're working now, not just flopping down the street like a pet.

Cart pulling? Even better. This is what they were bred to do—literally. Draft work is in their bones. It activates something ancient in them. Teach a Rottie to pull a cart and you'll see it click. The chest comes up. The focus tightens. You get less goof, more grit. Doesn't have to be a big rig. Start with something small. PVC carts exist. DIY rigs work too. What matters is teaching them the mechanics, giving them resistance, and letting them pull under command.

Here's the part most owners miss: Rottweilers thrive under structured effort. Not chaos. Not free-for-alls. Not tossing a ball until their tongue hangs out. They need effort with rules, with an outcome, with a clear boundary for success and failure. That's why problem-solving games hit so hard for them. Not flashy ones. Not overpriced puzzle feeders that your dog solves in ten seconds and then flings across the room.

Real problem-solving means friction. Make them think. Make them struggle a little. Put their food in a cardboard box and tape it shut. Hide scent objects under bowls and make them figure out which one holds the reward. Stuff their meals into a towel and roll it tight like a burrito. Make them use their nose and paws and brain instead of just their mouth.

This is where you stop thinking like a toy catalog and start thinking like a working dog handler. If it's too easy, it's boring. If it's too hard, it's frustrating. But if it's *just* challenging enough to make them work for it? That's where the magic is. That's when your dog starts self-regulating. That's when their eyes stay soft. Their pacing slows. Their focus returns. Because you let them chase something hard and win.

And no, you don't need to spend $300 on enrichment gear to do this. You don't need a subscription box. You need a cardboard box. An old towel. A freezer. Some peanut butter. A muffin tin. Some damn creativity. Throw some treats in a box, stuff it with junk mail, close the lid, and let your dog destroy it to get the reward. Roll kibble into a beach towel and let them unroll it with their face. Freeze a bone broth-soaked rope toy overnight. Drop it in the yard and let them wrestle it into submission.

It's not about being clever. It's about keeping them engaged without needing to supervise a circus. Enrichment isn't always cute. Sometimes it's messy. But it's also what keeps them from chewing your baseboards and dragging the throw pillows into the backyard like trophies.

But enrichment isn't just toys and jobs. Sometimes it's **real work**—the kind humans rely on. Therapy. Service. Search and rescue. These roles aren't for everyone, but when they're right, they're perfect.

Therapy work gets overlooked for this breed because people assume they're too serious. Too intense. Too "scary." Bullshit. A well-bred, emotionally stable Rottweiler makes an unbelievable therapy dog. Calm. Grounded. Present. Walks into a hospital or a memory care facility and the whole room changes. That deep eye contact? That solid body? People feel safe around them when they're handled right. They don't yap. They don't fidget. They just *are*. And sometimes that's exactly what people need.

Service work is a harder bar, but it's real. Rottweilers with the right temperament and training foundation make excellent mobility and PTSD service animals. They're large enough to provide support. Smart enough to learn complex task chains. Grounded enough to tolerate pressure. Not every Rottie is built for this—hell, most aren't—but when you get one who is, the bond goes beyond pet ownership. It becomes symbiotic.

Search and rescue? That's another level. Drive. Endurance. Obedience under chaos. If your dog's got the genetics and you've got the time, SAR is an outlet that gives back to the world while pushing your dog to their edge. Wilderness tracking. Urban disaster recovery. Human remains detection. These jobs aren't cute. They're not for Instagram. But they are one hell of a way to honor what this breed was built for—work that matters, work with consequence.

But here's the catch. You can't wait until your Rottie is bored and twitchy to start adding this stuff. Enrichment has to be built into their daily structure, not thrown at them when shit hits the fan. You don't hand a dog a Kong and call it enrichment while ignoring the rest of their needs. You build routines around mental effort the same way you build them around meals, exercise, and sleep.

And if you skip it? You'll know. You'll see it in the pacing. The sudden reactivity. The disobedience that looks like attitude but is really just a dog that hasn't had to think all week and is now unraveling from the inside.

That's the mistake people make. They assume a trained dog is a fulfilled dog. But training is just control. It doesn't feed the working part of the brain. It doesn't scratch the itch. And when that itch festers, it doesn't matter how many titles they've earned or how pretty their heel is—they'll find something to do. And it will suck.

But when you do this right? When you build work into the week? Real work—not just "be cute"—the difference is insane. You get a dog that's not just obedient, but *satisfied*. You get softness where there was tension. Calm where there was edge. You get predictability, because your dog doesn't feel like a firework in a shoebox anymore. You built the fuse line. You gave the spark somewhere to go.

This is what separates handlers from owners. Handlers think beyond the walk. They think about how to build a life the dog can thrive in. They don't treat enrichment as an afterthought. They treat it like air.

Because in this breed?
It fucking is.

CHAPTER SEVENTEEN: END-OF-LIFE CARE & SAYING GOODBYE

No one wants to write this chapter. No one wants to read it. But if you own a Rottweiler, you're going to live it. That's the deal. They give you everything. You pay with heartbreak. If you can't handle that, don't get the dog.

This breed doesn't age slowly. There's no gentle glide into the sunset. They don't grow old the way golden retrievers do, with greying muzzles and a limp that just means they're "slowing down." Rottweilers decline like they lived—fast, hard, and without warning. One day they're charging the yard with full force, and the next, they hesitate before jumping into the truck. Then they stop altogether. Then it's the stairs. Then it's the walks. Then it's everything.

It comes in waves, not a steady slope. One good day makes you think you overreacted, but then three bad ones stack up like bricks, and you realize that "he's just tired" isn't cutting it anymore.

The first signs are small. The pause before lying down. The shake in the back legs. The way they stop chasing the ball halfway and just walk back, like they're pretending they didn't really want it. The tail still wags. They still want to be near you. So you lie to yourself. You say it's not time. Not yet.

But here's the truth: **Rottweilers will follow you into the fucking fire** if you ask them to. They will wag their tail through the pain, because they don't want to let you down. They will try to stand when they shouldn't, try to eat when it hurts, try to be "good" when they're falling apart inside. They're not fine. They're loyal. And that's not the same thing.

Pain can be managed. But suffering? That's what happens when you convince yourself there's still time, even when the evidence is all over your floor. When your dog struggles to stand after sleeping. When they cry out trying to poop. When they start slipping on hardwood and avoiding the stairs because they're afraid they won't make it back up. When their breath comes shallow and their eyes start glazing over even though they're still trying to find you in the room.

You start tracking their decline in your head like a horror story you can't admit you're part of. You count the meals they skipped. You watch how their breathing changes at night. You start logging vet visits like court dates. You're waiting for the moment you can say, *"Now. Now it's bad enough."* But by the time you say that out loud, you've probably waited too long.

The cruelest part? There's no clear line. No alarm goes off. Just a thousand tiny moments where the dog who used to own every room they entered becomes a ghost in your hallway. And they know it. You can see it in the way they look at you. That flicker of confusion. That slow, tired gaze that says, *"What do you want me to do?"*

You can't pretend not to see it. Not if you actually give a shit.

So here's the part no one tells you until it's too late: start making a list while they're still well. Write down everything that makes their life *theirs*. Chasing a ball. Jumping in the car. Running to the door when you get home. Climbing stairs without help. Eating with enthusiasm. Going on walks without stopping. Wagging their tail when their name is called. Write that shit down. And as the list starts shrinking, you'll know.

When only one or two things are left, you don't wait until those are gone too. That's not love. That's cowardice wrapped in grief. You're not waiting for peace—you're hiding from responsibility.

The day you realize they're still alive but not *living* anymore? That's the day you make the call.

And making the call? It's going to fucking hurt. Worse than anything else. You'll pick a date and time and then spend every minute until then watching them like it's a countdown. You'll question yourself a hundred times.

You'll look for signs that maybe they're okay. Maybe it's too soon. Maybe you're being dramatic.

You're not. You're doing the hardest, kindest thing you'll ever do.

Let's talk about the part no one wants to say out loud: the **logistics of death**. Because it's not like the movies. There's no warm glow and perfect closure. You're going to have to decide where it happens—at home, or in the clinic. You're going to have to decide what happens to the body—cremation, burial, private, group, ashes or not. If you're smart, you're planning this *before* you're sobbing into your steering wheel with your dog in the backseat.

In-home euthanasia is worth every fucking penny if you can afford it. They don't have to be scared. They don't have to walk into a building that smells like sterile fear. They get to fall asleep on their bed, with your voice in their ear and your hand on their chest. They don't get shoved into a cold room. They don't spend their last minute hearing a receptionist answer the phone.

You think the moment of death is the worst part. It's not. It's what comes next. The silence. The leash still hanging by the door. The bowl you can't bring yourself to move. The phantom sounds—you'll hear them anyway. You'll think you see them in the corner of your eye. You'll hesitate before stepping over the spot where their bed used to be. Your routine will keep stuttering because your muscle memory still expects to be followed from room to room. You'll still say "be right back" to the empty house.

And if you have other dogs? Get ready. They know. They'll sniff the bed, search the yard, stare at the door. Some will act out. Others will shut down. They won't eat the same. They won't move the same. That pack structure just lost a pillar, and they feel it—same as you.

And you're going to feel like shit. Because even if you did everything right, your brain will try to eat itself with doubt. "Was it too soon?" "Did I miss something?" "Was there another treatment?" "What if we'd tried acupuncture? CBD? That supplement from that group online?"

Stop. You did enough. You ended their pain before they forgot who they were. That's what matters.

Let me tell you what *doesn't* matter: the opinion of anyone who says "it was just a dog." If someone says, "you can just get another one," they don't understand what these dogs are. What they cost. What they give. What it means to build a relationship with something that would rather die than disappoint you. If someone wants to rush your grief, tell them to fuck off. This is your story, not theirs.

Eventually, maybe you'll start thinking about another dog. You'll feel guilty about it. Like you're replacing the one you lost. You're not. That dog? That one was singular. Irreplaceable. But you're not trying to fill their space. You're honoring what they taught you. You're carrying forward the lessons you earned through blood, sweat, and ugly sobbing.

You'll do better next time—not because you failed, but because now you know. You'll catch the signs earlier. You'll structure the days smarter. You'll build the routine tighter. You'll never again say "I didn't know." Because you do now. You paid the price. You earned the wisdom.

And still—it'll hurt. Years later. You'll be driving, and a song will come on, and you'll fucking lose it. You'll find a ball under the couch and feel like you just got punched. You'll meet someone else's Rottie and feel your throat close. That's the cost of loving a dog like this. You don't just miss them. You miss the version of yourself that existed only when they were around.

So here's the deal. If you made it to the end, and you held the line, and you let them go while they still knew they were loved—you did it right. Even if it broke you. Especially if it broke you.

Because that's what it means to love a Rottweiler all the way to the end.
It's not easy.
It's not clean.
It's not peaceful.

But it's the most honest thing you'll ever do.

And if they could speak, they'd say it back:

"Thanks for not letting me suffer. Thanks for carrying the weight when I couldn't. Thanks for walking me all the way home."

CHAPTER EIGHTEEN:
RESCUE AND REHABILITATION

I didn't go looking for another dog. In fact, I'd promised myself—out loud, to actual humans—that I was done. After my last Rottweiler, a brick-headed, furniture-eating freight train named Loki, I'd sworn off starting over. I'd had enough of the puppy chaos, the shredded drywall, the endless debates with trainers, vets, and well-meaning strangers who all seemed to think they knew my dog better than I did.

So when I found myself scrolling late one night through the adoption listings for local shelters, it wasn't because I was ready. It was because I wasn't sleeping. And staring at dog faces on a screen seemed marginally less self-destructive than texting my ex.

Then I saw him.

No name. Just "Male Rottweiler, est. 3–5 years, no history." The photo was grainy, taken through a chain-link fence. He looked straight at the camera—head low, eyes darker than I was ready for. You could tell just by looking: this dog had seen some shit. His ears were set back, not in fear, but in something else. A kind of waiting. Like he'd stopped expecting anything and wasn't surprised anymore when nothing came.

I told myself I was just going to ask. That's how it always starts, doesn't it?

The shelter was in the next town over, tucked behind an old feed store and guarded by a gate that clearly hadn't been opened without a fight in years. The woman at the front desk—Margie, I think—warned me three separate times that this dog wasn't "pet material." Said he'd been found roaming in a vacant lot, no collar, no chip. They'd patched him up from some kind of scrap with another animal and he hadn't warmed up to a single volunteer.

"He's not aggressive," she said, eyes narrowed. "But he's not...safe. Not yet."

Perfect, I thought. I'm not safe either.

They brought me to his run. He didn't bark. Didn't growl. Didn't move. Just stared. Heavy stare, like he was trying to see if I was going to flinch.

I sat down on the concrete. Not close. Just within range. "You don't have to like me," I said. "But I'm here."

And maybe it was my imagination—or maybe it was something real—but I swear he exhaled just slightly, like a muscle behind his eyes unclenched by half an inch.

I took him home three days later. No fanfare. No Instagram post. Just me, the dog, and the long silence of a car ride where neither of us had any idea what we were about to walk into.

The first few days were a blur of containment. I'd prepped, of course. Gated rooms, a crate in the bedroom, food, slow-intro plans, vet appointments lined up in pencil. But all of that meant nothing when I opened the car door and he refused to come out. Not refused with fear. Not panic. Just stillness. A total absence of urgency. Like he had no reason to believe that whatever was outside the car was better than what was inside it. I didn't force it. Just sat there and waited.

Ten minutes passed before he shifted forward. Another two before he stepped out. By the time we got to the front door, I knew I was in it.

He didn't sniff around or explore. He found the far corner of the living room, curled up behind the recliner, and closed his eyes. That's where he stayed for the next five hours.

No accidents. No destruction. No barking.

I should've felt relieved. I felt sick. Because that wasn't a calm dog. That was a dog who'd shut down.

People think the first sign of trouble is aggression. It's not. It's quiet. The dog that makes no sound, no eye contact, no move to investigate? That's a dog that's been taught the world is a thing to survive—not engage with. That's a dog who learned early that movement got punished.

I named him Rex, mostly out of irony. He didn't respond to it. He didn't respond to much of anything.

At night, I left the crate open, set a soft bed beside it, and slept in the hallway. Not for him—for me. I didn't want to leave him alone. I didn't want him to wake up in another place full of more rules he didn't understand. He didn't cry. He didn't pace. He didn't sleep either.

By day five, he was eating, drinking, and peeing outside— but only if I left the back door open and went inside. He didn't take food from my hand. He didn't follow me from room to room. But he also didn't growl. Didn't flinch. He was there. That was all. And honestly, at that point, I counted that as a win.

The first time he let me touch him was accidental. I was sitting on the floor with my back against the wall, reading a training manual I didn't believe in, and he walked past me—close enough that his tail brushed my arm. He didn't startle. He didn't stiffen.

So I tried again the next day. Reached out, slow and low, palm up. He sniffed. Backed off. No teeth. No snap. Just distance.

On day ten, he let me scratch behind his ear. Ten seconds, maybe less. And I cried like an idiot.

Rescue dogs don't give you a training plan. They give you a puzzle missing half the pieces. You try something, watch it fail, and then try something else. You celebrate things that shouldn't need celebrating—eating near you, falling asleep while you're in the same room, playing with a toy without freezing when you look their way.

I didn't introduce him to anyone for almost a month. Didn't take him on public walks. Didn't try to have a friend over. Didn't even attempt a vet visit. I just let him live. Let him learn my rhythms.

I'd turn on the coffee maker; he'd move from one side of the couch to the other. I'd open the fridge; he'd stand up and leave the room. Every sound had meaning. Every movement, a trigger.

And I kept thinking—what the hell did they do to you?

But I never asked out loud. Because it didn't matter.

What mattered was who he became next.

There was a moment—maybe six weeks in—where I thought, *We've turned the corner.* He met a friend's neutral female dog on a parallel walk and didn't react. He let me put a leash on without ducking. He sniffed the neighbor's kid through the fence and didn't retreat.

It was working.

Until it wasn't.

At week eight, something shifted. He started growling when I approached his food bowl—not every time, just occasionally. He stiffened when I reached toward his collar. And one night, as I bent to pick up a piece of dropped food near his bed, he lunged.

Didn't connect. Didn't bite.

But the sound—the flash of teeth, the warning bark that rattled through the walls—sent me straight back to that first week, heart hammering, throat dry.

He backed off the second I stepped away. Lay down. Whined, like *he* was the one who'd just been startled.

And that's when it hit me: I'd mistaken silence for peace. Stillness for progress.

But this wasn't regression. It was revelation.

He wasn't getting worse. He was finally feeling safe enough to show me who he really was.

That's the thing no one tells you when you adopt a rescue Rottweiler. The honeymoon ends when the real dog shows up. And sometimes the real dog is messier than the one you picked up from the shelter. Sometimes they're guarded. Defensive. Overwhelmed.

And you have to decide, in that moment, whether you're ready to meet them where they are.

I backed up. Reset. Called a behaviorist who didn't flinch when I used the word "guarding." We built new routines. New thresholds. Reinforced trade games. Rethought touch protocols. And slowly, again, Rex let me in.

We had setbacks. Rainstorms he couldn't handle. Trash trucks that made him collapse into the corner. One terrifying vet visit that ended with sedation and an apology from the tech who'd "never seen a dog panic like that."

But we had wins too.

He started playing. He started seeking contact. He started offering behaviors—sits, downs, even a clumsy paw target we never really mastered. He started to look like a dog again.

And one day, while I was sitting at my desk, he came over and laid his head in my lap. I didn't move. Didn't say a word. I just let it happen.

It's been almost two years now.

Rex still doesn't like strangers touching him. We manage public spaces carefully. We work the muzzle like it's just another piece of gear, not a sign of shame. He's still not what I'd call "bombproof."

But he's mine.

And I know him.

I know when he's tired. I know when his back hurts. I know the exact sound he makes when he sees something he doesn't understand but wants to. I know the way his tail wags slow when he's unsure but willing to try anyway.

He's never going to be the dog who gets invited to breweries or curled up on the couch with a crowd of kids.

But he is the dog who follows me from room to room now. Who waits at the door when I leave. Who leans in for ear scratches with a sigh that sounds like home.

And if you asked me—was it worth it? Every setback. Every scar. Every hard decision. Every behavior consult. Every hour spent on decompression walks and desensitization drills and the days where I thought, "Maybe I'm not the right person for this dog."

Yes.

A thousand times yes.

Because he's not the same dog I brought home.

And maybe I'm not the same person either.

Most people think rescue starts when the dog gets adopted. That moment in the parking lot when the leash changes hands, the paperwork gets signed, and the new owner poses for a photo with a caption like, "Welcome home, Bear!" But that's not the start—not even close.

It starts weeks, sometimes months, before that feel-good photo ever gets posted. It starts when someone at animal control calls a rescue coordinator and mutters, "We've got a stray Rottweiler. Intact male. No chip. Picked up near the highway. No visible injuries, but... he's not great." That's usually all you get. A vague summary and a silent understanding that if this dog doesn't leave soon, he's not going to leave at all.

So the scramble begins.

A volunteer agrees to make the hour-long drive. They load the crate, bring gloves, and toss in a can of spray cheese just in case. At the shelter, they find a big black dog in a cold kennel—dirty, trembling, eyes wide and vacant. He's been there a few days, and in that time, no one has seen his tail wag. He doesn't growl, doesn't approach the gate, doesn't eat unless no one's looking. He's not shut down; he's floating. Distant. Survival-mode. You can see it in the way he flinches when the leash gets clipped. The volunteer doesn't say a word. They just load him into the crate, close the door, and drive.

That car ride is the first moment of decompression. There's no talking, no music, just quiet. A covered crate. A calm driver. A dog who doesn't understand what's happening but understands it's different than the last few days. When they arrive at the foster home, it's already prepped—double baby gates, lockable crate, water bowl, a single blanket in the corner. No kids. No introductions. No forced affection. Just space.

Because real decompression isn't two days of snuggles and a new name. It's three weeks—minimum—of doing less. Less eye contact, less petting, less trying to be "the good guy." You don't start obedience. You don't test thresholds. You don't invite the neighbor over to meet him. You don't rush a walk because the dog seems bored. You let the nervous system come down. You let the adrenaline drain. You observe. And if you're lucky, you get one moment—a glance, a soft blink, a quiet breath—that tells you he's starting to land.

But most people don't have that kind of patience. And even fewer have the skill to know what they're looking at when they finally get it.

Is that dog just shy, or is he dangerously conflict-avoidant? Is he barking because he's scared, or because he's testing boundaries and about to escalate? The average dog lover can't answer those questions. The average foster doesn't have the tools. So that's when the rescue calls in the behaviorist—not the ones from YouTube, not the influencer with 300k followers and a spray bottle—the real ones. The ones who show up with steel-toe boots, a clipboard, and body language so neutral it practically vanishes into the wall.

They don't ask for "sit." They don't do food lures. They don't play with toys or toss treats. They observe thresholds. Reaction to pressure. How long the dog recovers after a startle. What happens when you take away escape routes. How fast the tail stops wagging when you apply light social pressure. They're not testing for tricks. They're testing for safety.

And then they give you the truth.

Sometimes the truth is encouraging. "He's avoidant but not dangerous. He'll come around with time and structure. Keep stimuli low, start confidence building, give him a clear routine."

Sometimes it's hard. "He's safe, but not stable. No kids. No small animals. Needs an experienced handler. Strong muzzle conditioning required."

And sometimes it's the kind of truth that nobody wants to say out loud. "He's a bite risk. No clear warning signs. Shows avoidance until he doesn't. And when he breaks, it'll be fast, and it'll be bad."

This is where rescue gets real. And this is also where most people want to look away.

Because the internet loves to say "all dogs deserve a second chance," but the internet doesn't show up to court when that second chance goes wrong. They don't sit with the rescue director at midnight while she tries to decide whether to invest resources in this one dog—or save four others with clean slates and time to spare. They don't pick up the pieces when a foster gets bitten. They don't explain to donors why the "rehab case" had to be euthanized after six weeks of progress and one unpredictable outburst. They just repost the feel-good story and scroll on.

Meanwhile, back at the rescue, people are breaking. Fosters are burning out. Behaviorists stop answering their phones.

Volunteers ghost because they can't keep their hearts from breaking every time they open their inbox.

And the dogs? The dogs wait.

They wait in kennels. In crates. In temp homes. In the spare rooms of people already stretched thin. They wait to be understood. To be seen. To not be punished for the fear someone else put into them.

Some of them make it. Some find homes that really do the work. Who follow decompression protocols. Who don't treat affection like a shortcut to trust. Who understand that stability doesn't come from cuddles—it comes from consistency.

But a lot don't. Not because they weren't good dogs. But because the damage done to them takes more than love. It takes time, knowledge, and support. And most adopters show up with love and not much else.

That's why we lose them.

Because they came in feral. Or shut down. Or on their third return because the last two adopters thought "he just needs time" but didn't give him a plan. Because he bit someone in a moment of panic. Because he barked too much. Because he didn't connect. Because he didn't trust.

And what nobody tells you is that trust is the last thing to come—and the first thing to break.

Rehabilitation isn't a training plan. It's a nervous system reset. You're not just teaching sit and stay. You're teaching, "You're safe now." Over and over, until the dog believes it. Until the tension leaves their shoulders. Until the eyes go soft. Until they stop flinching at kindness. Until they stop bracing for pain. Until the leash isn't a threat. Until food isn't currency. Until they stop testing if you're going to leave.

That takes more than a rescue story and a hashtag.

It takes structure. A literal physical structure—crates, gates, pens—and the mental kind: rules, routine, restraint. Not because the dog is bad. But because the dog doesn't know what else to do. Because no one ever taught them what safe looks like. Because chaos is familiar, and familiar feels safe, even when it isn't.

It takes experience. To know when to push and when to pause. To see that the barking is fear, not defiance. That the snapping is confusion, not dominance. That the pacing isn't excitement, it's a stress response. That the silence isn't calm—it's collapse.

And it takes a kind of emotional grit most people don't realize they need until they're in too deep. Because this kind of work will wreck you. Not once. But over and over again. And the only way through is to remember that your heartbreak is not more important than the dog's healing.

The reward?

It's quiet.

A head rested on your foot. A tail wag when you walk in. A soft sigh in the crate when they finally sleep through the night without whining. A single calm look in a room that used to send them spiraling.

That's the work.

Not for everyone. But for the ones who get it, who really get it—it's the most brutally beautiful thing they'll ever do.

And yet, even after all that truth, after all that effort, here's the hardest pill to swallow: some people still think adopting a rescue dog is the "easy option." That it's a noble shortcut. That it's the fast lane to a grateful companion who knows they've been saved and will behave accordingly.

That fantasy dies quick.

Because rescue isn't about fixing a broken dog with hugs and hot dogs. It's about starting from zero—or below—and building something new with a creature who has every reason not to trust you.

People like to imagine that rescued Rottweilers come with a kind of poetic gratitude. They don't. Not right away. Sometimes not ever. What they come with is baggage. Sometimes visible. Sometimes buried so deep it won't show until month four, when their guard drops and the real dog steps forward. That's the moment you find out what you've really adopted. And by then, the leash is in your hand. The promise is made. The dog is yours.

So before anyone gets too far down the romanticized road of "saving a life," they need to pause and ask a different question: can I carry this one?

Not just when it's going well. Not just when the dog is sleeping peacefully in the sun. But when the leash turns into a liability. When the vet won't take them out of the backseat without sedation. When the neighbors stop waving. When the dog snaps at a family member, or freezes in the kitchen for the third time this week and won't move.

Because that's part of it too. The setbacks. The fear. The moments when love isn't enough and you have to lead even when you're terrified yourself.

It's not a failure to admit you're not ready. It's a kindness. To the dog. To yourself. To the people who will clean up the pieces if you get it wrong.

But if you are ready—really ready—it can be the most worthwhile thing you've ever done.

Not glamorous. Not convenient. But real.

A dog that comes to you not because you chose the perfect puppy, but because you saw the broken pieces and said, "I'll stay anyway."

And stayed.

And proved it.

Every single day.

Until that dog—against every odd—believes you.

That's not rescue. That's resurrection.

And you don't get it by accident.

You earn it.

One moment at a time.

CHAPTER NINETEEN: LEASH IN HAND

If you've made it this far, congratulations.

No, really—congratulations. Because this book wasn't designed to coddle you, flatter your feelings, or sell you a fantasy. It was a war map. A dossier. A hard look at the truth behind the cute photos and bite-sized videos.

You've read about the price, the pressure, the panic. You've walked through the early chaos, the mistakes, the blood-on-your-forearms phase. You've stood in the ruins of a destroyed living room and still come back the next day with a leash and a plan.

That means something.

It means you didn't flinch when it got ugly. It means you didn't bail when the dream didn't match the reality. It means you're still here—on the other side of the noise—with the leash in your hand and your feet on the ground.

That's where real dog ownership begins.

Not the day you pick up the puppy. Not the day the adoption is finalized. Not even the day the dog stops peeing in the crate or chewing the doorframe. The real beginning happens the moment you realize this isn't just about training a dog.

It's about becoming someone worth following.

See, Rottweilers don't worship you. They don't roll over just because you raised your voice or waved a treat. They are loyal—but not blindly. They follow—but not without reason. They challenge what's unclear. They test what's weak. They question everything, and they remember what you show them, not what you say.

They make you earn it.

Not once. Every day.

And that's what sets this breed apart. It's not the size. It's not the bark. It's not the bite force that people love to obsess over in comment sections. It's that these dogs, if you raise them right, will mirror back your choices with brutal accuracy. You want clarity? Lead clearly. You want trust? Be consistent. You want obedience under pressure? Build the reps when it's easy. You want calm in chaos? Show them what calm looks like.

There are no shortcuts here. No hacks. No secret collars or miracle commands. Just time, presence, and a standard you don't drop, even when it's inconvenient. Especially when it's inconvenient.

Because that's what real leadership is. And that's what this breed demands.

They don't want a buddy who spoils them. They don't need a tyrant who controls them. They need a partner. Someone who understands that boundaries are a kind of love. That trust is earned in the quiet moments. That pressure must be fair, not constant. That control without communication is just coercion.

You don't "own" a Rottweiler. You live with one. And if you do it right, you move through life like a unit. Like a pair. Like something forged, not found.

And if you screw it up?

They'll let you know.

They'll shut down. Or they'll explode. They'll chew the leash, dodge your hand, flatten their ears, widen their eyes, growl under their breath. They'll push back. Because they are not soft. They are not passive. They are not wired to be endlessly tolerant of human chaos. You either become worthy of their trust, or you pay the price for skipping steps.

It's not cruelty. It's clarity.

And it's the reason this breed doesn't belong in just anyone's hands.

That's not gatekeeping. That's protection. For the dogs. For the public. For the people who pick up the pieces when things go sideways.

Because when a Pomeranian bites someone, it's funny. When a Rottweiler does, it's a lawsuit. A headline. A death sentence.

These dogs carry the weight of every myth ever told about them. The movie villain. The junkyard menace. The unpredictable monster. And every time one of us screws it up—doesn't train, doesn't lead, doesn't prepare—that myth gets louder. Stronger. Deadlier.

That's the weight we carry as Rottweiler owners. Not just the dog at the end of our leash, but the reputation of the whole breed.

It's not fair. But it's real.

So we train. We socialize. We supervise. We proof commands. We reinforce calm. We structure freedom. We build confidence. We muzzle train. We crate condition. We don't hope things go well—we stack the odds.

Because we understand the deal.

These dogs give you everything—if you show them how to channel it. They will lay down their lives for you, stand between you and the world without hesitation, and ask only that you give them a reason to believe you'll do the same.

And that's the part people don't get until they've lived it.

This isn't just about obedience or safety or keeping your furniture intact. It's about who you become in the process of raising a dog like this. The version of yourself that learns to slow down. To think. To lead without ego. To show up, again and again, even when you're tired, even when you're frustrated, even when no one else would blame you for quitting.

That version?

That's who your dog sees.

That's who they trust.

And when you earn it—truly earn it—it's unlike anything else. You won't need praise. You won't need a ribbon. You'll just look at your dog in a crowded place, off-leash, surrounded by chaos, and you'll say their name.

And they'll come.

Because you built that.

Because you were there for the 3 a.m. crate training and the land-shark phase and the reactivity meltdowns and the heartbreak of setbacks and the grind of rebuilding. Because you didn't flinch when it got hard. Because you trained in the rain. Because you did the boring reps when no one was watching. Because you told the breeder no when the red flags showed. Because you walked away from the backyard litter. Because you said no to the easy version and yes to the real one.

You did this.

You made this dog.

And in doing so, you made something else: a legacy.

Because Rottweilers don't just leave fur on your couch and holes in your drywall. They leave an imprint. On your routines. On your worldview. On your sense of responsibility. On your spine.

They sharpen you.

So here you are, at the end of the book, and maybe the beginning of something else. Maybe you've already got your dog. Maybe you're still waiting. Maybe you've got one in the crate next to you right now, chewing through their fourth leash this month.

Wherever you are, this is your moment.

Not to "figure it all out." Not to have perfect answers. But to commit. For real. To say, "Yes. I'm in. I'll do the work. I'll keep showing up."

Because that's the only promise that matters to your dog.

Not that you'll never mess up.

Just that you won't disappear when you do.

So take the leash.

Walk forward.

You've got a Rottweiler now.

And they're watching.

WELCOME TO THE BEST & WORST DECISION OF YOUR LIFE.

So. You made it through.

You read the warnings. You slogged through the gear lists, the bite stories, the financial landmines, the behavioral breakdowns, the emotionally raw rescue truths—and you're still here.

Still thinking this breed might be for you.
Still looking at your bruised arms and shredded hoodie like, *yeah, worth it.*

Still saying, "Okay, what's next?"

Here's what's next:
You either rise to the occasion… or your Rottweiler falls through the cracks.
There is no middle ground with this breed. No "just wing it." No "they'll grow out of it."
They grow *into it*—into the behavior you allow, into the leadership you offer, into the environment you shape.

If you screw it up, they don't just become annoying.
They become dangerous.
Not because they're bad dogs—but because they are strong, smart, pressure-sensitive working animals built for intensity.
And if you fail to give them clarity, structure, and purpose, they'll invent their own—and you'll hate the results.

But…

If you get it right?
If you push past the chewed baseboards and the public judgment and the behavioral chaos of adolescence—
If you learn to lead like your dog's sanity depends on it (because it does)—

If you advocate, train, supervise, and sweat through the hard parts without giving up?

You'll get a dog unlike any other.

Not a "good pet."
Not a couch accessory.
But a partner.
One that watches you with hawk eyes and follows you into storms.
One that reads the room before you even open your mouth.
One that knows when to drop the ball and when to stand their ground.

You'll get the dog who makes people stare.
Who makes cops roll their windows down and say, "Damn, that's a Rottweiler?"
Who makes other handlers whisper, "How the hell did you train that?"
And the truth is: You didn't *just* train that.
You earned it.
Every scar. Every rep. Every midnight cleanup, every meltdown, every moment you chose to correct instead of coddle, to show up instead of shut down.

You *became* someone that kind of dog could trust.
Someone worth following.
Someone who *deserved* a Rottweiler.

That's the part nobody tells you.

You're not just raising a dog.
They're raising you, too.

So here's your final mic-drop:
If this book scared you off?
Good. It should have.
Rottweilers aren't for everyone.
And the people who *shouldn't* own one? They'll read the first two chapters and nope out.

But if you're still standing at the end of this?
Still saying, "Let's go"—with eyes wide open and leash in hand?

Then welcome.
You've made the best worst decision of your life.

And we wouldn't have it any other way.

Appendix A
New Owner Survival Checklist

If You're Missing These, Return the Dog.

You made it through the cute photos, the "good with kids" sales pitch, and the fantasy that love alone would get you through puppyhood. Cool. But now the real test starts: **are you actually prepared to keep this dog alive, sane, and out of court?**

Here's your **no-excuses checklist**. If you don't have these things—or don't plan to get them this week—you're not ready. You're a liability with a leash.

Gear You Actually Need (No, the Cute Collar Doesn't Count)

Crate – Sturdy, appropriately sized for a full-grown Rottweiler. Divider panel required. This is not optional unless you enjoy drywall confetti and ER vet bills.

Ex-Pen or Gated Play Area – Your "open floor plan" is not a training environment. You need zones. Zones save lives.

Leashes (3) – One durable 4–6 ft for daily walks, one 15–30 ft long line for training, one backup in your glove box for emergency GTFO moments.

Flat Collar with ID Tag – Name, your number, no cute slogans. You're not auditioning for TikTok.

Harness or Slip Lead – Based on your training approach, not aesthetics. Know how to use it—or don't use it at all.

Muzzle – Properly fitted, well-conditioned. Because prevention > PR disaster. If your dog ever gets scared, injured, or too excited, you'll be glad you have it.

Treat Pouch – Clip-on, washable, big enough to hold high-value bribes. If you're not training, you're regressing.

Training Treats – Soft, smelly, non-crumbling. You'll go through these faster than you think.

Toys (Durable AF) – Kongs, rubber bones, rope toys. No squeaky plush unless you want to feed it to them in pieces.

Damage Control Supplies

Poop Bags – Stockpile. Everywhere. In every jacket, car, drawer.

Enzymatic Cleaner – For accidents, barf, mystery puddles. If it doesn't say "urine destroyer," it's not strong enough.

Bitter Apple or Anti-Chew Spray – Won't stop all destruction, but might save your baseboards.

Baby Gates – More than one. Block off problem areas before the problems start.

Slow Feeder Bowl – This dog is not a vacuum. Don't let them eat like one.

Health and Medical Prep

Vet Appointment Booked – Within the first 72 hours. This isn't just a checkup—it's triage.

Vet Records and Breeder Info on File – Microchip number, vaccine history, emergency contact. If something goes sideways, you need fast answers.

Pet Insurance Activated – If you don't have this by day one, you're playing financial Russian roulette.

Emergency Vet Contact Saved – Know your nearest 24-hour clinic. Drive the route. Save the number.

Training and Structure Tools

Hired Trainer or Consult Booked – Before the problems start. You are not "just winging it." Not with this breed.

Puppy Plan or Training Schedule – Feeding times, potty schedule, nap structure, training sessions. Routines keep dogs calm. Chaos builds reactivity.

Place Cot or Training Mat – For teaching impulse control and off-switches. Yes, you need one.

Clicker (Optional but Smart) – If you're doing marker training, don't rely on your voice when it's shaking with frustration.

Paperwork and Reality Insurance

Breeder or Rescue Contract – If there wasn't one, that was your first red flag.

Proof of Vaccinations and Microchip Registration – You'll need this when a neighbor complains or if your dog slips a leash.

Photos of Dog from All Angles – In case they go missing. Don't rely on one Instagram-ready headshot.

Current Homeowner/Renters Insurance Policy – Double check breed restrictions and liability clauses. Some companies don't cover Rottweilers. Know before someone files a bite report.

Things You Think You Don't Need (But Absolutely Do)

Quiet Space for Decompression – Dogs aren't furniture. They need retreat zones. If your house is chaos, your dog will be too.

Time Off Work for First Week – Puppies need structure. Rescue dogs need decompression. Your job can wait. The critical bonding window cannot.

Back-Up Care Plan – If you break your leg, get sick, or need to travel. Who's handling the dog? If the answer is "I dunno," you're not ready.

If you're looking at this list and thinking, "Well, we don't need all of that…"

Return. The. Dog.

Seriously.

Because this isn't a wishlist. It's your *bare minimum*.

This breed doesn't reward good intentions. It rewards preparation. Clear leadership. Absolute follow-through.

You don't need to be perfect. But if you're unprepared?

You won't just fail.
You'll fail hard.
And your dog will pay the price.

So, stock up. Get serious. Build the damn fortress.

The storm's coming.

Be ready.

APPENDIX B
TRAINING & SOCIALIZATION TIMELINE

If You Miss These Windows, You'll Be Cleaning Up for Years

There are no do-overs in Rottweiler development. You miss a window; you don't get it back—you get to wrestle with the consequences instead.

So, here's the **condensed reality** of what your dog should be learning, when, and why skipping these steps is the fastest route to a muzzle, a lawsuit, or a rehoming ad that starts with "He's a good boy, BUT…"

Let's go.

Puppyhood (8 to 16 Weeks)

Theme: Foundations or Failure
This is not the cuddle window. It's the neural network construction zone.

Name + Recall:
By 9 weeks, they should whip their head around when you say their name. No delay. No guessing. Reward it like you're giving away gold.

Crate & Alone Time:
Crate conditioning starts *immediately*. Not "once they settle." Now. Also: start short bursts of alone time. Rottweilers bond hard. You must train separation.

Potty Schedule:
Religious. Every 30–60 mins when awake. Rewarded. Tracked. If you screw this up now, you'll be smelling it for months.

Socialization (with rules):
Not chaos. Not flooding. Controlled exposure to:

Strangers of all sizes/ages
Other dogs (vaccinated and calm)
Sounds, textures, surfaces
Vet clinics and groomers
Positive + neutral experiences only. One meltdown now =
months of reconditioning later.

Muzzle & Handling Work:
Start it. Normalize it. Touch paws, ears, teeth, tail. Muzzle
condition like it's a standard tool—because it is.

Basic Obedience:

Sit
Down
Touch (targeting)
Name recognition
Engagement (look at me = treat)
If they don't know what "yes" or a marker means by 12
weeks, you're already behind.

4 to 6 Months

Theme: Adolescence Begins. Bite Now or Bleed Later.
Hormones are whispering. Drive is increasing. And that
baby brain? Starting to push boundaries. **

Leash Manners: Start structured walks. Pulling now = a
freight train later. If they lunge at squirrels, fix it before
they outweigh you.

Place Command: Impulse control in real life. Use it during
dinner, guests, chaos. Reinforces calm > crazy.

Handling Rehearsals: You want a dog that doesn't need
sedation for a basic exam? Practice the handling drills.
Daily.

- Nail trims
- Ear cleaning
- Vet holds

Neutrality to Strangers and Dogs: Your goal is calm
indifference. Not obsession. Not "he just wants to say hi."
That ends in disaster. You're not raising a greeter.

Play & Prey Management: Redirect biting and mouthiness into controlled play. Structured tug, flirt pole, fetch. No chaos games, no face-grabbing. No chasing kids.

Training in Public: Short sessions. Controlled. Calm exits if overstimulated.

- Pet stores
- Sidewalks
- Parking lots
- Busy corners

Start Threshold Respect: No door dashing. No bolting out of crates or cars. Respect is built in seconds—not corrected in emergencies.

6 Months to 1 Year

Theme: The Betrayal Phase.
The dog who used to listen now looks you dead in the eye and ignores you. Welcome to real adolescence.**

Reactivity Watch: Fear periods hit like landmines. Sudden barking at shadows? Growling at hats? This is where owners screw up with punishment. Don't correct fear—build confidence. Redirect. Reward recovery.

Advanced Obedience: Proof these in chaos. Not your living room.

- Recall under distraction
- Sit/stay in motion
- Down from a distance
- Place with duration
- Leave it

Start Real Boundaries: No more free-roaming indoors. Earned freedom only. Default should be crate, leash, or supervised.

Impulse Control Drills: If your Rottie doesn't know how to "do nothing," you'll have to teach it—with reps.

- Food refusal

- Waiting at doors
- Chill around guests

Neutral to Chaos: Your job now is not to test your dog, but to read them. Farmer's markets? Airports? Family BBQs? Introduce wisely, not for Instagram.

Start Guarding Management: Resource guarding is preventable—but only if you *actively* condition sharing. Train out food, toy, and space aggression before it blooms.

1 to 2 Years

Theme: Power with Purpose
The body's mature. The mind is calculating. You either have a partner now—or a power struggle waiting to happen.**

Structured Lifestyle: Training is now your lifestyle—not a "session." Your dog's brain is watching *all the time*:

1. Do you follow through?
2. Do you reward the right things?
3. Do you ignore little problems until they're big?

High-Level Distractions: Train in the real world. Bus stops. Sporting events. Busy trails. You want your dog to hold a down-stay when a skateboard flies past? That's not luck. That's reps.

Proof Recall Under Pressure: If you can't call them off another dog, a squirrel, or food on the ground, your dog is a liability.

Protective Instinct? Channel It: Rottweilers mature slowly. At 18–24 months, that deep guardian drive kicks in. If you haven't built trust, clarity, and neutrality by now, you'll be managing a dog that makes its own calls.

Muzzle Work Maintained: Even if you don't "need" it now, keep the conditioning. Emergency vet visits, pain responses, or public panic will happen. Your dog's life might depend on your prep.

Training Tune-Ups with a Pro: Even the best trainers need outside eyes. Do a check-in with a behaviorist or working-dog trainer. Catch holes before they crack wide open.

Fitness + Mental Work: Your Rottweiler is a working breed. Couch potato life = behavior problems. Regular:

- Obedience
- Tracking
- Scent work
- Agility
- Pack walks
- Structured play

Exhaustion ≠ enrichment. Give them a job.

Final Note: Milestones ≠ Finish Line

Your dog will be learning every single day of its life. What changes is *what they're learning from you*. Are they learning to respect pressure and find calm? Or are they learning that you're inconsistent, emotional, and easy to ignore?

Structure isn't cruel. It's clarity.
Boundaries aren't punishment. They're safety.
And training isn't about control. It's communication.

Rottweilers don't need perfection.
They need **leadership with a spine**.

Miss the timeline, and you'll spend years undoing what you should have prevented.
Stick to the timeline, and you'll build a dog that doesn't just look good on a leash—but trusts you with its life.

And acts like it.

QUICK REFERENCE: HEALTH RED FLAGS

Vet NOW vs. Google Later

Let's make this easy: **Rottweilers are tough.** Which is why when something actually *is* wrong, it's usually serious. You don't get second chances with bloat. You don't get to "wait and see" when a 120-pound dog suddenly can't stand.

So here's your **panic guide**:
☑ = **Vet NOW** — no calls, no Google, no "wait an hour."
❗ = **Monitor + Act Soon** — but don't sleep on it.
💬 = **Google Later** — annoying, weird, but probably not fatal today.

If you're unsure? Always assume the worst and call your vet.

Collapse, Weakness, or Sudden Immobility

☑ Rear legs give out suddenly
☑ Dog won't or can't stand
☑ Coordination lost (staggering, leaning, eyes darting)
☑ Screaming in pain when trying to move
☑ Dragging back legs with no resistance

❗ Possibilities:

- Spinal injury
- Tick paralysis
- Hemangiosarcoma rupture
- Degenerative Myelopathy (if chronic)

🐾 **ACTION:** Carry, don't walk. Immediate vet. This isn't going to pass.

Bloat (Gastric Dilatation-Volvulus aka GDV)

☑ Restless pacing + drooling
☑ Trying to vomit but nothing comes up
☑ Distended, tight abdomen
☑ Suddenly anxious, then lethargic
☑ Collapse or shock symptoms

⏳ You have **minutes**—not hours. Every second counts.

⚕ **ACTION:** Emergency vet NOW.
Call on the way. Tell them you suspect bloat. Skip the "wait and see" phase. If you're wrong, great. If you're right, delay = death.

Sudden Lethargy + Pale Gums

☑ White or grayish gums
☑ Won't get up, even for food or walk
☑ Cool limbs, glazed eyes
☑ Collapse or fast shallow breathing

❗ Possibilities:

- Internal bleeding (ruptured spleen or tumor)

- Shock

- Cardiomyopathy

- Severe anemia or blood loss

⚕ **ACTION:** Vet NOW.
Pale gums are not "tired." They're "circulatory system failing." This is not normal. Don't Google—go.

Bleeding: When to Panic

☑ Blood spurting or pulsing
☑ Deep wound through muscle
☑ Muzzle/gum trauma + blood
☑ Bleeding from nose, rectum, or coughing blood

❗ Small surface cuts that stop bleeding with pressure = 💬 Google Later
☑ Anything arterial, internal, or unexplained = Vet NOW

⚕ **ACTION:** Muzzle if needed, apply pressure, get moving.

Breathing Issues

☑ Gasping, choking, blue tongue/gums
☑ Wheezing with panic
☑ Open-mouth breathing while resting
☑ Labored, heaving breaths while not active
☑ Collapse after excitement

❗ Possibilities:

- Heatstroke

- Tracheal obstruction

- Laryngeal paralysis

- Cardiac failure

- Allergic reaction

🐾 **ACTION:** Immediate vet if breathing is *changed and panicked* or *blue gums appear*.
If panting seems excessive but the dog is responsive and cools off with rest, monitor. But don't take chances.

Seizures

☑ Whole-body convulsions
☑ Loss of bowel/bladder
☑ Unresponsive during or immediately after
☑ Cluster seizures (more than 1 in 24 hours)
☑ Long recovery or aggression post-episode

🐾 **ACTION:** First seizure ever = Vet NOW
Known seizure dog = track time and clusters
Cluster or prolonged seizure = emergency vet

😴 Brief "twitches" during sleep or dreaming? That's fine. Let them chase dream-squirrels.

Limping or Sudden Lameness

❗ Limp with no weight-bearing = See vet within 24 hrs
😴 Occasional limp with no pain = Watch 1–2 days
☑ Sudden scream and refusal to use limb = Vet NOW
☑ Joint swelling, heat, or visible deformity = Vet NOW

❗ Possibilities:

- ACL tear

- Elbow/hip luxation

- Fracture
- Infection in joint

🐾 **ACTION:** If they scream, limp, and won't touch the leg = don't wait. Don't "see how it looks tomorrow."

Neurological Weirdness

☑ Sudden aggression with no trigger
☑ Running into walls or circling
☑ Eyes flicking side to side (nystagmus)
☑ Head tilt + loss of balance
☑ Zoned out or "not there" mentally

🐾 **ACTION:** Vet within hours
Could be vestibular, stroke, brain tumor, toxin. None of these are a DIY problem.

When to Google Later

☺ Reverse sneezing
☺ One-time vomit after eating too fast
☺ Normal-colored soft poop
☺ One skipped meal in a dog who's otherwise fine
☺ Eye boogers
☺ Excessive shedding (welcome to Rottweiler life)
☺ Zoomies at 10 p.m.

Final Rule: If You're Asking "Is This an Emergency?"

…it probably is.
If you're holding your dog and *hesitating* between calling the vet or scrolling Reddit?

Just. Call. The. Damn. Vet.

It costs nothing to ask.
It costs everything to wait.

If You Forget Any of This, Don't Expect Your Dog Back Intact

Leaving your Rottweiler with someone else—whether it's a sitter, family member, pro trainer, or boarding kennel—isn't just about packing food and saying "he's good with people." This is a breed that *requires structure, management, and clarity*, even when you're not the one holding the leash.

So here's your **non-negotiable checklist**.
If it's not in the bag or the notes, don't hand over the leash.

Packing List

Must-Haves (or cancel your trip):
Crate – Full-sized, familiar, and labeled. If they're not crate-trained, they're not ready for boarding.
Food – Pre-portioned, labeled by meal. Don't make people guess how many scoops. Include backup kibble in case of spills.
Treats – High-value AND familiar. Don't assume the sitter knows your dog's diet or allergy triggers.
Leashes – One short control leash, one backup. No retractables. No frayed "emotional support" leashes from 2012.
Flat Collar + ID Tags – Name, number, and ideally "Needs Structure" as a warning label.
Training Tools – Slip lead, prong (if trained on it), e-collar (if trained), harness—*whatever they actually use daily*. Don't pack gear they don't know.
Medications – Labeled with dosing, written instructions, vet contact.
Vet & Emergency Info – Folder with rabies certificate, recent health records, and emergency clinic address.
Toys/Chews – 2–3 max. Familiar, safe, durable. No plush.

Nothing new or untested.

Muzzle – Even if they're perfect. Vet emergencies happen. Pack the muzzle they've been conditioned to wear.

Cleaning Supplies – Enzymatic spray, poop bags, wipes. Don't make your sitter hunt for paper towels at midnight.

Sitter/Boarding Instructions

Print this. Or hand-write it. But **leave it behind**. No instructions = all liability is yours.

1. Feeding Schedule
• How many times per day?
• How much per meal?
• Any "wait before play" rules (bloat risk)?
• Allergies? Forbidden foods?

2. Medications
• Dosage, time of day, what to do if missed
• Any behavioral meds or anxiety treatments?
• Signs of overdose or reaction to watch for?

3. Behavior Cliff Notes
• People-neutral or protective?
• Dog-friendly, selective, or NO DOGS?
• What triggers them? (hats, delivery trucks, skateboards?)
• Any past aggression, reactivity, fear behavior?
• Leash manners: are they trained, or a land shark?

4. Commands They Actually Know
List them. And what they *mean*.
(Not just "place"—but "go to your mat and don't move until released.")
Include marker words: "Yes," "Good," "No," "Break," etc.

5. Daily Structure
• Usual wake-up time
• Crate schedule
• Walk times
• Play/training windows
• Nap/quiet time
Structure helps regulate stress. Mimic the home routine where possible.

6. Emergency Protocols
• Closest 24-hour vet (with map link if needed)
• Authorization form (who can approve treatment if you're unreachable)

- Backup contact with decision-making power
- Transport plan: where's the crate? Who can lift them?

7. Handling Rules
- Do NOT reach into crate.
- Do NOT remove food bowls mid-meal.
- Use leash/collar protocols as trained.
- Muzzle if unsure—**no shame, just safety.**
- Respect body language—if they freeze, back off.
- Don't introduce to new people or dogs unless pre-approved.

8. Signs of Stress or Medical Red Flags
- Refusing food for more than 1 day
- Excessive panting while resting
- Vomiting more than once
- Loose stool + lethargy
- Unusual aggression or withdrawal
- Excessive drooling, pacing, shadowing
- Sudden reactivity that wasn't there before
= **Call immediately.**

Don't assume your Rottweiler is "easy" just because *you* know how to manage them.
Sitters don't have your timing, your voice, or your intuition. Give them tools, not just tasks.

If your dog's training is shaky, your crate routine inconsistent, and your behavior notes full of "he usually doesn't…"
→ You're not ready to board. Stay home.

But if your dog has structure, clarity, boundaries, and you've left nothing to chance?
Go enjoy your trip.
They'll be waiting for you—whole, sane, and mostly intact.

Appendix E
Emergency Contacts Page

Because No One Wants to Google "Dog Ate Tylenol" at 2 a.m.

In a real emergency, you don't want to be scrolling through texts or digging through email chains trying to remember your vet's weekend number or the name of that one trainer who knows your dog isn't "just being dramatic."

This page is your command center. Fill it out. Print it. Screenshot it. Stick it somewhere obvious.

Primary Veterinarian

Clinic Name: _____

Vet Name (if applicable): _____

Phone Number: _____

After-Hours Instructions: _____

Address: _____

Email (if used for scheduling): _____

Client ID #: _____ (if clinic uses one)

Notes: (Closed on weekends? Only open 9–5? Write it.)

24/7 Emergency Vet (ER Clinic)

Clinic Name: _____

Phone Number: _____

Address (with directions/landmarks): _____

Estimated Drive Time: _____

Notes: (Require deposit? Known wait times? Parking weird?)

Poison Control

ASPCA Animal Poison Control:
📞 1-888-426-4435 (Available 24/7)
💵 *Fee may apply at time of call*

Pet Poison Helpline:
📞 1-855-764-7661
🌐 www.petpoisonhelpline.com
💵 *Fee required—credit card needed*

If dog ingests a household substance:
What did they eat?
When did they eat it?
How much (roughly)?
Dog's weight?
Any symptoms yet?

Tip: Take photos of the product label + your dog. You'll need both.

Dog Trainer / Behaviorist

Trainer Name: _____
Business Name: _____
Phone Number: _____
Email: _____
Website/Socials: _____
Specializes in: (Reactivity, obedience, working breeds, etc.)

Availability for emergency behavior consults (Y/N)?
_____

Backup trainer contact (if applicable): _____

Emergency Backup Contacts

1. Local Friend/Family (has keys to house):
Name: _____
Phone: _____
Knows dog? (Y/N) _____
Can transport to vet? (Y/N) _____

2. Emergency Boarding/Foster Option:
Name/Facility: _____
Phone: _____
Has crate/training info? (Y/N) _____

3. Pet Insurance Info (if applicable):
Company: _____

Policy #: _____

Phone/Claim Line: _____

Portal login: _____

Notes & Quick Facts

Dog's Full Name: _____

DOB / Age: _____

Breed: _____

Microchip # / Company: _____

Spayed/Neutered? (Y/N) _____

Weight (approx.): _____

Vaccination status: _____

Known allergies: _____

Medications: _____

Behavioral Flags (circle):

- Fearful

- Leash Reactive

- Muzzle Trained

- Not Dog-Social

- Guarding Issues

- Needs Crate

- Flight Risk

- Medical Fragility

- Bite History

Special Handling Notes: _____

_____

Pro Tip: Keep a printed version in your glovebox, dog go-bag, and taped inside your pantry door.
Save a digital copy in your phone's "favorites" or notes app.
Share it with sitters, family members, and your trainer.

This isn't overkill. This is preparedness.
Because the day you need it isn't the day you want to *start* writing it.

Appendix F
Recommended Resources

Real Trainers, Real Books, Real Help—No YouTube Gurus, No Junk Science

This breed doesn't forgive bad advice. Whether it's training methods, health info, or breed-specific guidance, Rottweilers need structure, clarity, and handlers who give a damn about doing it right.

The following is a vetted (pun intended) list of resources—places we actually trust, people who've worked with power breeds, and organizations built around *doing the work*, not selling snake oil.

Breed & Working Dog Organizations

American Rottweiler Club (ARC)
www.amrottclub.org
→ The national parent club for Rottweilers under the AKC. Find breed-specific health info, breeder referral lists, and working event calendars (herding, carting, IPO, etc.). If you're serious about the breed, this should be your starting point.

United States Rottweiler Club (USRC)
www.usrconline.org
→ Focused on the working Rottweiler. Great resource for Schutzhund / IPO titles, breeding standards, temperament tests, and preservation breeders. Less fluff, more function.

AKC Canine Good Citizen / Trick Dog / STAR Puppy
www.akc.org
→ Solid frameworks for foundational obedience, manners, and public access readiness. Not the be-all-end-all, but a great place to start with structure and goals.

Local Schutzhund / IGP Clubs

→ Not all will accept beginners, and not all deserve your dog. Visit, observe, ask questions. Good clubs will focus on **clarity, balance, and relationship—not ego or force.**

Trainers & Organizations That Know Working Dogs

These are individuals or training companies that understand what it means to work with high-drive, thinking breeds like Rottweilers. No glitter. No treat-pouch-only delusion. Just reality-tested education.

Michael Ellis School for Dog Trainers

https://michaelellisschool.com/
System-based, pressure-aware training that emphasizes communication, motivation, and timing. Not a magic bullet—just damn good instruction.

Ivan Balabanov

www.trainingwithoutconflict.com
Controversial to some, respected by many. Focuses on clarity and motivation with working breeds. Best for handlers ready to go deep into theory.

Jeff Gellman / Solid K9 Training

www.solidk9training.com
Balanced trainer known for working with high-reactivity dogs and owners at their wit's end. Not everyone's cup of tea, but battle-tested in behavior cases.

Grisha Stewart (BAT 2.0)

www.grishastewart.com
Best resource for **fear, aggression, and reactive dogs—** especially adopted adults with trauma history. Less obedience, more emotional rehab.

Must-Read Books (No Woo-Woo BS)

"The Culture Clash" by Jean Donaldson

A classic. Understands how dogs think—and how we get in their way.

"Raising Your Puppy With Love and Leadership" by Michael Ellis

Direct, structured, and reality-based—especially helpful for working breeds.

"Don't Shoot the Dog" by Karen Pryor
Sometimes over-hyped, but still foundational for anyone using reward-based systems.

"Dog Training for Dummies" by Jack & Wendy Volhard
It's old-school—but clear. Good for total beginners.

"Pit Bull: The Battle Over an American Icon" by Bronwen Dickey
Not about Rotties specifically, but a brilliant dive into breed bias, fear culture, and media myths. Must-read for anyone owning a "scary breed."

Real Websites (You Can Bookmark Without Regret)

PetMD
www.petmd.com
→ Decent first-stop for general health info. Just don't substitute it for a vet.

DogFoodAdvisor
www.dogfoodadvisor.com
→ Independent reviews of dog foods with recall alerts. Not gospel, but a good research start.

Veterinary Partner
www.veterinarypartner.vin.com
→ Vetted (by vets) health library. Use this for deep dives into conditions your Rottie may face.

Whole Dog Journal
www.whole-dog-journal.com
→ Bit crunchy, but strong on holistic care, supplements, and behavior from a thoughtful perspective.

Companion Animal Behavior Program – UC Davis
https://ccab.ucdavis.edu/behavior
→ Gold standard behavior science and vet-backed behavior protocols. Excellent for serious behavior cases.

What to Avoid (Because We Love Your Dog)

-Instagram "trainers" with nothing but flashy heel work and no pressure tools

-YouTube clicker cults that swear "positive-only" fixes everything
-Breeders who don't compete, don't title, and say things like "I've never needed health testing"
-Forums full of angry pet parents bashing every trainer with actual accountability
-Reddit for anything but emotional support and memes

Final Tip: Build Your Personal Resource Binder

Print articles. Save vet records. Keep gear receipts. Make a "dog drawer" with:

- Vaccine schedule
- Training plan
- Food/water schedule
- Emergency contacts (see Appendix E)
- Boarding instructions (Appendix D)
- Adoption records or breeder contract
- Muzzle training notes
- Vet discharge paperwork
- Insurance policy
- Favorite trainers' phone/email

ABOUT THE AUTHOR

Zero Woofs Given was born out of one sarcastic human's lifelong gripe with the sugarcoated nonsense in dog books. Founded by Shannon, a snarky, lifelong dog devotee and proud Rottweiler mom to Rowan and Rip, has spent 20+ years knee-deep in fur, mud, training sessions, and vet clinic exam rooms, surviving the kind of chaos only a determined canine can create. From rescue work to breed-specific research, she's seen the best, worst, and most unhinged sides of dog ownership and lived to write about it.

Shannon's mission is blunt: when people pick the wrong dog, the dog pays the price. They end up in shelters for being exactly what they were bred to be—while humans fail them. Her guides exist to stop that cycle.

Zero Woofs Given Press exists for one reason: to torch the sugarcoated garbage. These books won't tell you every dog "loves kids" or "thrives in apartments." They'll tell you the messy, hilarious, heartbreaking truth—so you know what you're getting into before your shoes, furniture, and sanity are destroyed.

When not writing, she's wrangling her own four-legged disasters, dodging drool, and questioning life choices while still believing there's no better companion than a dog with a heartbeat and zero manners.

THANK YOU

Thanks for picking up this book and giving it your time, energy, and probably a few coffee-stained evenings. Writing honest breed guides isn't about selling you a fantasy—it's about making sure you know what you're really signing up for when a Rottweiler (or any dog) bulldozes into your life.

If this book saved you from one bad decision, helped you understand your dog better, or at least made you laugh while your Rottie drooled on the couch, then it did its job.

Want more of this kind of brutal honesty? Sign up for *The Feral Dispatch* newsletter at ZeroWoofsGiven.com. It's the only place you'll get fresh doses of unfiltered dog truth, weekly chaos, and the occasional reminder that your dog is normal—it's the humans who are messed up.

And while you're there, check out the rest of the Zero Woofs Given Dog Breed Library. Every guide is just as blunt, just as sarcastic, and just as likely to save your furniture and your sanity.

And if you've decided maybe a Rottie isn't for you but you still want a peek at other breeds, hit our Dog Breed Profile page on the website. It's packed with early-access snippets of guides still in the works—so you can get the unfiltered truth before the full book drops.

So thanks for showing up for the raw version, not the sugarcoated bullshit. You're the reason this series exists—and maybe the reason your Rottie doesn't eat the neighbors.

REFERENCES

American Kennel Club. (n.d.). *Rottweiler Dog Breed Information*. https://www.akc.org/dog-breeds/rottweiler/

Andrew. (2014, August 4). *Outdoor Activities For Your Rottweiler | RottweilerHQ.com*. RottweilerHQ. https://www.rottweilerhq.com/outdoor-activities-for-your-dog/

Breed Standard: Rottweiler | United Kennel Club (UKC). (n.d.). https://www.ukcdogs.com/rottweiler

Carting With Your Dog - Positive Draft Training for Fun and Competition. (n.d.). Dogwise. https://www.dogwise.com/carting-with-your-dog-positive-draft-training-for-fun-and-competition/

Dog Sports Rottweilers Can Participate In. (n.d.). https://www.oocities.org/rottweilersrus/dogsports.html

DogTime. (2024, July 2). *Rottweiler*. DogTime. https://dogtime.com/dog-breeds/rottweiler

How To Care For Rottweilers | VIDA Veterinary Care. (2022, April 6). VIDA Veterinary Care - Denver & VIDA Veterinary Care - Centennial. https://www.vidavetcare.com/dog-breed/rottweiler/

Hughes, L. (2023, October 17). The Ultimate Rottweiler Puppy Ownership Guide. *Pawrade.com*. https://www.pawrade.com/resource/breed-highlights/the-ultimate-

rottweiler-puppy-ownership-guide?utm_
source=google&utm_campaign=&utm_medium=ad&utm_
content=&utm_term=&gad_
source=1&gclid=CjwKCAjw6c63BhAiEiwAF0EH1AUmHB
OHVDdFXSM-
NGbIotuFeCpol4e7xvb3LRLXq9W1XiK2jqQZfRoCEwwQ
AvD_BwE

If you love this breed this is the place for you! (n.d.). https://
www.reddit.com/r/Rottweiler/?rdt=39939

Jackson, M. (2024, September 4). *What Is Schutzhund? A Comprehensive Guide to the Incredible Dog Sport.* Dogster. https://www.dogster.com/lifestyle/what-is-schutzhund

Mph, H. N., DVM. (2024, April 19). *Rottweiler.* https://
www.petmd.com/dog/breeds/rottweiler

Niles, A. (n.d.). *American Rottweiler Club – AKC National Rottweiler Breed Club.* American Rottweiler Club. https://
www.amrottclub.org/

North American Flyball Association | About Flyball. (n.d.).
https://www.flyball.org/aboutflyball.html

Piper, G. (2024, September 5). *What Are the Top Dog Sports & How Can I Participate? A Complete Guide.* Dogster.
https://www.dogster.com/lifestyle/top-dog-sports

Rottweiler | VCA Animal Hospitals. (n.d.). Vca. https://
vcahospitals.com/know-your-pet/dog-breeds/rottweiler

Rottweiler Hearts Rescue. (2022, July 18). *Home - Rottweiler Hearts Rescue.* Rottweiler Hearts Rescue - Rottweiler Hearts Rescue (RHR) in North Carolina Region Dedicated to Rescue and Rehabilitation of Rottweilers. RHR Does Not Breed or Sale Rottweilers. https://rottweilerheartsrescue.
org/

Rottweiler Rescue Foundation. (2024, August 15). *Supporting U.S. Rottweiler Rescue Groups - Rottweiler Rescue Foundation*. https://rottweilerrescuefoundation.org/

Schutzhund Training - United Schutzhund Clubs of America. (2013, October 3). United Schutzhund Clubs of America. https://www.germanshepherddog.com/about/schutzhund-training/
United States Rottweiler Club. (n.d.). *United States Rottweiler Club*. https://www.usrconline.org/

Wikipedia contributors. (2024, August 31). *Rottweiler*

Wikipedia. https://en.wikipedia.org/wiki/Rottweiler